Starting Your Own
RESTAURANT

D0533094

SARA RIZK

Starting Your Own

RESTAURANT

All you need to know to open
a successful restaurant

SARA RIZK

crimson

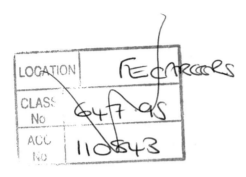
This edition first published in Great Britain 2008 by
Crimson Publishing, a division of Crimson Business Ltd
Westminster House
Kew Road
Richmond
Surrey
TW9 2ND

A catalogue record for this book is available from the British Library.

ISBN 978 1 85458 436 6

Printed and bound by Mega Printing, Turkey

Contents

Introduction

f you've picked this book up you, at some point, have had dreams of running
your own restaurant. Perhaps you have a passion for food, or you're the best
party host among your circle of friends. Whatever the cause of your ambition,
it's one shared by thousands of others. Restaurants are a source of pleasure and
entertainment for millions around the world and, if you're a regular diner, you
may want a slice of the action from the other side of the kitchen.

The aim of this book is to provide you with the inspiration to actually turn
your dream into a real-life thriving restaurant. However, it should also help you
understand what a mammoth task starting a restaurant really is. It's not for the
fainthearted. You'll need guts, determination, and the ability to work around
the clock without flagging. You'll need to give up your social life, at least for the
first year. You'll have to say goodbye to your family, unless they're joining you at
the restaurant. Starting a restaurant will probably be the most exhausting and
gruelling endeavour you'll ever take on. If you're not prepared for that right now,
then perhaps you should put this book back on the shelf until you are.

Of course, that's the tough bit. The rewards can more than make up for all that
hard work. Simon Kossoff, founder of Carluccio's, summed up the experience of
being a restaurateur beautifully: 'I used to stand in the middle of a busy restaurant
and feel like I was running a party'. It's that buzz which will feed your ambition and
keep you on your feet serving your customers even when you're shattered.

Simon Kossoff and seven other restaurateurs have shared their experiences
in this book. You can find the individual stories of these successful restaurant
owners on pages 4-14, but there are tips and anecdotes from all of them
throughout the book. Iqbal Wahhab describes the nightmares he experienced
with budgets and overrunning building work when starting The Cinnamon Club.
Robin Rowland talks about the agony of having to close unsuccessful branches of
Yo! Sushi to save the company. There are also tips and real-life experiences from

restaurateurs you won't have heard about; dedicated individuals such as yourself that run businesses they've built from scratch.

Because you may not know where to even begin, this book takes you through the process step-by-step. Firstly, it's crucial to think through your idea, before you even spend a single penny. Everything from the type of restaurant you want to run and the quality of food you want to serve, to the future plans you have for the business need to be thought through right now.

The book will also guide you through the concept of identity, highlighting the importance of your restaurant's name, branding and reputation. For those of you who are a little apprehensive about the prospect of pitching for funding, there's a whole chapter dedicated to raising finance, which explains your various options and offers advice on presenting your idea to those holding the purse strings.

Getting your business plan spot on is a major part of successfully obtaining adequate funding and there's plenty of help with getting that sorted, as well as information on the kind of detail you need to include.

Moving on to section two there's help with every aspect of turning your idea into a reality. Not sure what kind of business structure you need to trade under? Read the chapter on registering your business to find out. If you've never written a press release or dealt with the media before, make sure you pay close attention to the chapters on launching and ongoing marketing. It's absolutely crucial too that you study the *Getting Legal* chapter so you're not caught out by the laws and regulations that govern the restaurant industry.

So that you can plan ahead, we offer plenty of advice on getting through your first few months of trading; from adapting your menu to managing your staff you need to ensure you run your restaurant like a well-oiled machine.

And for those of you who have big ambitions, what do you do once your restaurant is successfully up and running? Perhaps you want to turn your concept into a franchise, or float it on the stock market. You may even want to sell it on, and start something from fresh. All these options are covered in section four. While you may not be considering the future of your restaurant that far in advance, it's helpful to consider what may lie ahead.

So while your journey to become a successful restaurateur won't be an easy one, it will hopefully be extremely rewarding. The primary aim of this book is to give you the vital information you'll need, and to reassure you that although you'll undoubtedly come across hurdles, every restaurateur is in the same boat. With the experts' advice, you should be able to avoid some of the more crippling roadblocks, making your personal business journey that little bit smoother.

Case Studies

FROM THE EXPERTS

These experts have been there and done it, and turned their restaurants into a sensation. Simon Kossoff and Robin Rowland have turned Carluccio's and Yo! Sushi into national chains, successful in nearly every major city in Britain. Iqabl Wahhab, with his groundbreaking new Indian cuisine at The Cinnamon Club, and highly acclaimed British fare at Roast, began with a large ambition, and is now well known on the prestigious London restaurant circuit. Read about their restaurants here, and benefit from their expert advice throughout the book.

IN MY EXPERIENCE

These restaurants may not be national phenomenons yet, but they are certainly well positioned to give advice on opening a restaurant. Most of these restaurants have recently opened, so the start-up process is very memorable. Others have been in business for five or 10 years, enough time to build up a steady customer base, and have some great tips on marketing and survival to impart.

Carluccio's

Simon Kossoff
Type: Italian
Start year: 1999

Simon Kossoff attributes his career in the restaurant industry to a rebellion against the accountancy and marketing jobs all his university colleagues were taking after graduating from their economics degrees. Not wanting to follow suit, he enrolled on a new postgrad course he'd heard about – International Hospitality Management. It was the first step in a long career journey which eventually led him to Antonio and Pricilla Carluccio, and one of the most successful new restaurant concepts in the UK.

'I initially just wanted to be a student for another year', he says. With no available grants for the course he'd chosen, Simon supported his extra year of study by working in restaurants receiving what he describes as 'proper experience'. 'It's still the case, but it was even more so 30 years ago, that to get a career in the restaurant business you needed to have done your time washing dishes and serving customers. Simon's first job after finishing the course was in a large hotel in London, but it proved a decidedly unrewarding experience. Nine months later, Simon found himself at Pizza Express, under original founder Peter Boizot, when the number of outlets was in the tens rather than the hundreds.

Simon established a knack for sorting out management difficulties which led him to My Kinda Town, an American-themed company which ran hamburger and deep-dish pizza joints. The company was eventually sold to Capital Radio, and it was while working for the Radio Café that he met Antonio and Pricilla Carluccio.

The couple already ran a food shop in Covent Garden but Pricilla wanted to extend the business into an all-day casual restaurant. 'She wanted it to be something that could grow – more of a brand. She had a really clear idea of what she wanted but just didn't have the skills in her team to develop it, get funding and find the right sites etc. So we came together as a partnership.'

With the idea cemented, Simon and the Carluccios started the gruelling task of securing funding for a restaurant during the dotcom boom. 'I think it would have been easier for us to raise £200m for an online food venture than the £2m we needed for a bricks-and-mortar business. Pricilla and I must have done a hundred presentations, but the venture capitalists just weren't interested.'

After managing to secure some funding from business angels they met up with Seattle Coffee Company founder Scott Svenson. He had recently sold his company to Starbucks. Simon and the Carluccios had been trying to raise the required capital for nearly two years

but once Svenson came on board they had the rest of the cash within six weeks.

Simon had managed to keep a site near Oxford Circus on hold until the money came in. The investment documentation was signed on a Friday and the following Monday the builders set to work. It took 16 weeks to finish the first site, but each new Carluccio's is now finished in half that time. The first restaurant opened in November 1999 and was immediately very busy at lunchtimes, but empty the rest of the day. The all-day café theme was also not proving financially viable. They knew they'd either have to adapt the whole business model or go under.

'Pricilla had imagined it as a kind of Italian bar where you might pop in for an espresso and slice of pizza but she hadn't really viewed it as a restaurant. Over Christmas that year I rewrote the menu, put the prices up, added a breakfast menu and extended the opening hours so we could trade from 8am to 11pm.' Carluccio's first day of all-day trading was Valentine's Day 2000 and from that day onwards 'the whole thing just went insane'.

'We had people at breakfast, lunch and dinner. People came in for take away coffees and picnics. We'd gone from a fatally flawed business model to suddenly having the most exciting restaurant model any of us had ever seen.' The second site opened a year later in Fenwicks, Bond Street, after the department store approached them and even stumped up the cash to build it. 'That was great for us because they invested all the money, it was very close to our first site, and being in the store we had a captive audience.' However, it wasn't until the third restaurant that the business became sustainable. Although much bigger than originally intended by Simon, the St Christopher's Place restaurant was immediately very successful. 'It transformed the business from being one that was spending capital to one that was generating cash.'

Another £2m was then raised from the shareholders to expand further. By 2005, with 25 restaurants, the original investors were keen for Simon and the Carluccios to make good on their promise that they'd be able to realise their investment within five years. 'We had a few choices. We could have sold the business to another restaurateur or a private equity firm, but I felt the management team still had more to do, so we floated on AIM. I felt that at least that way we were in control of our own destiny.'

At the point of flotation Antonio and Pricilla sold the majority of their company share while Simon continued with the expansion. There are currently 35 Carluccio's restaurants but Simon believes there's scope for 100 in the UK, and is also starting to entertain the idea of international expansion.

FROM THE EXPERTS:

FROM THE EXPERTS:
The Cinnamon Club and Roast

THE CINNAMON CLUB

Iqbal Wahhab
Type: Modern Indian and traditional British
Start year: 2001, 2005

When Iqbal Wahhab decided to open his own restaurant, 'every restaurateur in London' told him he was crazy. Having come from a PR background he admits to never having served a single plate in a local curry house, let alone cooked anything in a professional environment. Most restaurateurs cite a long career in the industry as vital preparation for the difficulties that lie ahead, but Iqbal believes it was his lack of hands-on experience in the industry that made his first restaurant, The Cinnamon Club, such a success.

Although Iqbal hadn't directly worked in restaurants, his PR and publishing career had revolved around the industry. As well as representing several high-end eateries with his PR firm, Iqbal founded Indian restaurant trade magazine, *Tandoori,* in association with Cobra Beer. However, after some strong criticism of the way Indian restaurants in the UK were being run, he fell somewhat foul of the industry. 'They hounded me out', he says. 'It's hard to believe, but I had death threats. I had to go away, distance myself from it and open a restaurant of my own to show everyone what I was talking about.'

Iqbal had become tired of what he regarded as poor service and a lack of interest in the provenance of ingredients. 'I had seen from French restaurants the limitations of what the Indian restaurants at the very top were doing. There wasn't the same level of service or branding, let alone culinary direction, so I really saw a gap in the market.'

Armed with a novel concept, and the determination to prove his idea for a fine dining Indian restaurant could work, Iqbal now had to find the investors willing to fund the project, which proved trickier than originally envisaged. An initial site in High Street Kensington fell through as a result of funds not being secured for the lease. However, a new site in the Old Westminster Library then became available. 'Our biggest problem was convincing the landlord to give me the property. There were 300 people bidding for it so I wasn't exactly his last resort. I had to convince him he should give it to me over Conran, The Ivy or any of the others.'

Of the initial £2.5m needed to start the restaurant, Iqbal says only 'a tiny amount' came from his own funds. He needed a large chunk – around £1m – to come from the bank. As fate would have it, having already dreamt up the restaurant's name, he came across a bank manager called Paul Cinnamon. However, having secured the bank loan from the restaurant's namesake, Iqbal now needed to convince investors it was worth taking a chance on.

'Back then I didn't have a proper understanding of how to sell the idea. I'd hired an accountant who would come with me to presentations and do the numbers. But he didn't really know the restaurant trade and I soon realised he wasn't the one investors wanted to hear from. I found the more I got to grips with that side of it myself, the more encouraging the response from investors was.' The numbers weren't the only thing Iqbal lacked experience in. He dramatically underestimated the amount he would need to learn. 'I used to sit in meetings with architects, engineers and builders not having a clue what they were talking about but signing all the cheques.' Iqbal soon found himself £700,000 over budget and had to go cap-in-hand back to the investors. It's a mistake he didn't repeat when he opened his second restaurant, Roast.

After dodging several financial bullets, The Cinnamon Club opened its doors to the public in 2001 and despite turning over £2m in its first year the critics had some harsh words. There were accusations of 'ponciness', and the suggestion that Indian food simply didn't work when presented in the European template. Iqbal responded by fine-tuning the whole operation and insists the criticism gave him even more determination, eventually leading to respected restaurant guide Harden's describing it as 'London's best-known Indian'.

Despite The Cinnamon Club ultimately becoming a critical and financial success, the start-up phase had left some deep scars in the relationship between Iqbal and his investors. 'The relationship had gone from bad to dire with litigation on both sides. They had much deeper pockets to sue me so we agreed to a "drop hands" settlement.' In 2005 he walked away from the restaurant to set up Roast in Borough Market.

Iqbal describes Roast as 'traditional British food but not like you've seen it before'. The restaurant combines the finest quality ingredients to make classic British dishes in a beautiful setting and fine dining experience. Once again Iqbal had to fight off pitches from the top restaurant groups for the location – the Floral Hall at Borough Market, which overlooks the bustling stalls and sellers. But the concept of Roast fitted so well with the site's theme of great fresh produce, the market trustees were won over.

Having learned from his mistakes with the Cinnamon Club, the road to success wasn't quite so rocky the second time round and Roast has enjoyed praise from critics and diners alike from the outset. 'I wasn't going to let anyone pull the wool over my eyes this time so I learned all the unglamorous and tedious details. As a result we came much closer to hitting our budgets and deadlines.' Iqbal's time is now split between Roast, chairing a government advisory group on ethnic minorities and working with the Prince's Trust, but he isn't quite ready to give up the restaurateur's lifestyle yet. 'I'm starting to spend more and more time away from Roast, but I keep telling myself: "Open some more restaurants. You're good at it!."'

FROM THE EXPERTS:

FROM THE EXPERTS:
Yo! Sushi

Robin Rowland
Type: Sushi bar
Start year: 1997

Yo! Sushi had already established quite a name for itself by the time founder Simon Woodroffe handed over the reins to Robin Rowland. Back in 2000 when Robin was brought on as operations director the conveyor belt eatery had four London sites and was proving immensely popular with diners and critics alike, with well respected *Sunday Times* critic AA Gill describing it as 'the best sushi in London'.

Simon had opened the first restaurant three years earlier in Poland Street. It was quickly followed by a branch in Harvey Nichols, then at sites in Selfridges and Finchley Road. However, despite the popularity of the concept, the business had yet to find its feet financially. In 2001 Robin was appointed managing director and what followed was two years of cost cutting in an attempt to stay afloat. Robin's influence provided the commercial backbone to the company which has subsequently allowed it to grow to 40+ restaurants in the UK, with further sites in Ireland, Russia, Malaysia and the Middle East.

'At the time we had eight restaurants that weren't contributing on top of four successful ones. My job was to unpick that, get rid of three bars and three restaurants and at the same time, add another two. I knew I could grow the business but it would have to go through a difficult time before it became profitable.'

Robin says the biggest challenge was convincing the banks to believe in the project and not let it go bust. Another key obstacle was finding buyers for the restaurants that just weren't pulling their weight. 'The poor-performing sites were all about bad locations,' says Robin. 'The right thing to do was to get rid of the ones that couldn't be saved and nurse the others back to health in terms of management, standards and promotion.'

Robin's restaurant background had given him a solid grounding in developing successful roll-out concepts. A graduate training programme at Whitbread's (one of Britain's largest hospitality companies and one-time owner of TGI Friday's) saw him running 15 restaurants and pubs at the age of 22. 'Their philosophy was sink or swim, and they'd allow you to manage other managers. I ran everything from nightclubs to backstreet boozers. The hardest thing for me was managing people who were much older than myself, but it was a terrific experience. Their boot camp was a bit like the army.'

However, it was his time at southern American style chain Old Orleans that really taught him how to steer such a large hospitality group. Robin took the company to 24 sites in four years and says most of the management team he had at that point are now directors of restaurant businesses throughout the UK.

'Everything I've done at Yo!, most of the clues came from that business. While I was there I broadly worked out that there are only five things you need to focus on to have a successful business: making a profit, employing great people, creating a great product then promoting and publicising it.' Despite his fond memories of building up Old Orleans, Robin says his decision to join Yo! Sushi was born out of a desire to do something smaller. 'I went down a very corporate route in my 30s and had worked for large companies all my life. I wanted to work on something I had ownership of so I joined Simon, and within a year he took a step back.' Robin

says everything from the menu to the décor you see in Yo! Sushi now is down to his team. 'There's not really anything of Simon's original work. What he did was base the image around himself rather than the brand, but you can't really scale that as an idea outside of London.'

In 2003, with Robin at the helm, the company went through a management buy-out where Simon sold his controlling interest in the company to private equity firm Primary Capital. 'The buy-out took a year to pull off but we couldn't have grown the company without it. Simon had to be convinced that he could make more money out of a small piece of a large cake than a large piece of a small one.' That large cake is now on course to have a total of 60 restaurants by Christmas 2008, but the company has gone with a franchise route for the overseas sites. 'In my opinion you're off your rocker if you think you can make money overseas without help out there. I've seen so many companies arrogant enough to think they can do it with a great business model, but you can't do it without a reputation, an absolute knowledge of property and the right team out there.'

The acquisition of Yo! Sushi by private equity firm Quilvest in March 2008 was also influenced by a desire for international expansion. As well as providing an exit for the early Yo! investors, Robin says they've also found an internationally focused buyer. However, there'll be no branching out from the restaurant concept just yet. 'After an investment, you go for the most reliable means of return, so in the short-term we'll stick to opening restaurants in great locations that we know will be successful.'

Robin is now confident the company can continue to expand and his long-term goal is to have 100 restaurants by 2012. His buoyant outlook for the company is unfazed by mounting speculation over the current state of the economy. 'I've been here before, and in my experience, the good survive, the bad drop away and you'll see a clear divide between businesses which are overstretched and under financed and those with a great foundation and a good differentiator product. Yo! Sushi has a good formula for long-term success.'

Brown Sugar

Shevonne Bennett
Type: Modern Caribbean
Start year: 2007

Despite following a very corporate career path after leaving university, Shevonne Bennett knew the 9 to 5 lifestyle would never really be suited to her; it was the life of a restaurateur that truly called to her.

'Even when I was at uni, I remember thinking there were no decent Caribbean restaurants to eat in,' says Shevonne. She was frustrated that the only Caribbean places to eat in London were casual cafés rather than proper restaurants. Her vision was to take Caribbean food into the mainstream, allowing people from different cultures and backgrounds to sample it in a modern and sophisticated restaurant environment.

'I started writing my business plan while I was still in full-time employment.' Shevonne set herself goals to achieve in her planning. She got friends to look over her business plan and started attending marketing and business seminars whenever she could. 'I really felt that if I put my mind to it, I'd get the formula right. So I consulted people in the industry, and met chefs and restaurateurs at networking events.'

The branding of the restaurant was a big concern for Shevonne from the outset. She didn't want to create just one restaurant. She wanted a blueprint to take Caribbean cuisine to the masses and make it as popular as Italian or Indian food. As a result, she agonised over the name. 'I had some ideas in my head but none of them really fitted. Then one day I was watching a film called Brown Sugar and it just clicked.'

Once she had her plan finalised the next step was to approach the banks. 'I was denied funding again and again. Despite loving my business plan, they just couldn't see past my lack of experience.' Shevonne eventually found some private investors and used her parents as guarantors on a personal loan.

After finding a property in Clapham, South London, Shevonne opened Brown Sugar in February 2007 and it quickly became a hot hang-out. There was even some early press coverage. 'Getting in *Time Out* was amazing. They did have a few words of criticism, but they thought the food was tasty.'

However, Shevonne decided the site she occupied was too expensive. 'Our sales were really good and turnover has been really close to what we projected, but our outgoings were just too high.' Shevonne is now in the process of finding another site, and is relishing the opportunity to fulfil her long-term goal of building the Brown Sugar brand and educate the public about the delights of Caribbean cuisine.

IN MY EXPERIENCE:
The Duke of Cambridge

Geetie Singh
Type: Organic gastropub
Start year: 1998

Some entrepreneurs make a conscious decision to run their businesses ethically, even if it means foregoing a slice of their profits. But Geetie Singh has proved you can run a thriving business without sacrificing your core values. She opened her organic and environmentally sustainable gastropub the Duke of Cambridge in 1998.

'There are plenty of people running deeply ethical businesses and thinking their values through', says Geetie. 'But not many people are doing it in the restaurant industry'. The core values of the Duke of Cambridge aren't just about paying lip service to the concept of ethical trading in exchange for a few extra column inches either.

Having grown up in a commune where food origin and its environmental impact was a priority, Geetie was shocked at the lack of sustainability when she started working as a waitress. 'I couldn't understand how these chefs didn't have a clue what impact their food was having – lamb flown in from New Zealand, asparagus in December, battery hens. I knew there were people out there like me who wanted to eat in a restaurant knowing they were getting good quality, safe food that had a positive effect on society'.

After a decade in the industry, Geetie felt she had enough experience to open her own restaurant. Taking on partner Esther Boulton Geetie began her £250,000 fundraising mission. 'We started with banks we thought were least likely to say yes and practised on them. When we felt a bit more rehearsed, we moved on to the banks we thought we had a chance with'.

One bank agreed to lend them the money, and combined with the family loans and investment from a friend, they thought they'd secured the cash they needed. However, disaster struck three weeks before the launch when the bank called to say the paperwork hadn't actually been approved and they'd no longer be getting the cash. Some hardcore networking ensued and Geetie managed to raise the extra £100,000 the bank had originally promised from private investors.

After three premises agreements falling through, and funding problems, the Duke of Cambridge opened to a front page article in the *Evening Standard*. Geetie had budgeted for five people on day one. She ended up serving 30. The pub broke even in its fourth month and by the end of the year, was making a 'healthy profit'. In fact, profits have increased year-on-year since the launch. But Geetie says it's no longer about growth, it's about maintaining what she's built and ensuring her position in the market.

Gilgamesh

Ian Pengelley
Type: Pan-Asian
Start year: 2006

Having the high profile Gordon Ramsay Holdings pull the funding from your first restaurant isn't something most chefs would want to highlight on their CVs. But for Ian Pengelley, it marked a turning point in his career. In 2006, returning to prove both the media and his previous employer wrong, Ian opened Gilgamesh in Camden.

Ian left school with no qualifications. He'd come from a military family and grew up in Hong Kong before returning to the UK. He took a job in a country club 'washing pots and pans', but his first rung on the chef's ladder came at the expense of a colleague. 'One day the chef fired somebody. He turned to me and said, "get over here, you're cooking now".'

Despite the 16-hour days, Ian found he enjoyed the mix of creativity and discipline the kitchen gave him, and ended up staying for another two years. At the age of 21 he set off to the Far East and spent the next eight years learning the traditions and disciplines of oriental cooking.

At 29, Ian returned to the UK, having worked in China, Thailand, Indonesia, Australia, Vietnam and America. Such an impressive kitchen background caught the attention of Gordon Ramsay and negotiations began to open Pengelley's. The restaurant was a Pan-Asian concept with Ian in the kitchen and Gordon Ramsay Holdings bankrolling the venture.

'I was very young and very flattered, but I was slightly hijacked by the company. They chose the design and look of the place and all I was allowed to take care of was the food. The whole identity of the place was wrong. My style was laid-back Asian, and they did French. The two identities just didn't mix.'

Gordon Ramsay Holdings pulled the plug on Pengelley's less than a year later, and Ramsay has since listed the venture as one of his biggest mistakes. However, Ian doesn't share his sentiments. 'I don't regret it. It was a £1.5m training course with Gordon Ramsay.'

When the opportunity for Gilgamesh came along, Ian was in no mood to be bossed around again. 'I sat down with the manager on day one and told him I did not work for him. I was in charge of staff, the kitchen, the menu, the lot.'

Ian describes the first six months after Gilgamesh opened as hell. 'The spotlight was on us and I worked three months without a day off. The press wanted to know if it was going to be another Pengelley disaster.' Although there were some hiccups regarding service, Ian says he worked incredibly hard to perfect the menus and get the press on side. Gilgamesh is now consistently listed as one of London's coolest eateries.

Ian still spends most of his time at the restaurant, about five–six days a week. You need a good head chef before you can afford to step away from the restaurant, but I'm very proud of my team, my kitchen is sorted and I love my chefs.'

IN MY EXPERIENCE:

The Lounge

Eza Philippe Navaratnasingam
Type: Tapas bar
Start year: 2001

Philippe's restaurant career began at the tender age of 17 in Switzerland, where he took a job as a kitchen porter. Within three months he progressed to chef's assistant and what followed was an 18-year hospitality career culminating in his move to England in 2001 to set up Spanish tapas bar The Lounge. Philippe's experience ranged from serving politicians and investment bankers in some of the most prestigious restaurants in Zurich, to small family-run places in rural Switzerland.

Although Philippe found a property in South London he was very keen on, it was an arduous nine month process before he actually took possession of it. Philippe ploughed all his savings into the project, as well as taking out a loan for the lease and goodwill for the previous owners. Initial costs were kept low by using all of the existing furniture. Only the outside signage was changed to mark his new ownership.

The premises had originally been a bar and it showed. 'When we arrived, the kitchen wasn't even fit for domestic use. It consisted of an old burner, two old fridges and a freezer. I'd seen some shocking kitchens while looking for premises here but because I was new to the UK, I just assumed that's what London kitchens were like.'

Initially, the state of the kitchen meant Philippe could only serve a few snacks and had to run the business as a bar, but after six months he'd refurbished it to restaurant standards. He added 20 tapas dishes to the menu and took on a full-time chef. The gradual migration from bar to full-blown restaurant was successful and as the tapas menu expanded, turnover increased.

'Everything was going ok for a while but then the food quality started to dip and the balance sheets just weren't adding up. I wasn't in the kitchen so I couldn't tell if it was portion size, wastage or what. At that point I was in real financial trouble and I knew it was my last chance.'

Philippe kicked the chefs out and took over the kitchen himself with the help of some junior assistants. 'Since I've been running the kitchen I haven't had a single complaint about food quality, my profit margins and calculations are spot on, turnover is steady and food sales have increased 10% year-on-year.'

However, he admits such a hands-on role in the day-to-day running of the restaurant has taken its toll on home life. 'I've dreamt of running my own restaurant since I was 17, but now that I have this nice little business I realise it doesn't allow for a social or family life.

Sweet Mandarin
Lisa, Helen and Janet Tse
Type: Modern Chinese
Start year: 2004

The Tse sisters grew up submersed in the restaurant trade. Their family ran a Chinese restaurant and they'd often help out both in the kitchen and front of house. However, their own restaurant careers didn't blossom until much later but Lisa says she and her sisters always had an entrepreneurial streak.

It was a family trip to Hong Kong that sparked the idea for Sweet Mandarin. 'Our great grandfather was in the restaurant trade there, and it was on that trip that we really rediscovered our roots', says Lisa.

After returning to the UK, the sisters started to list the problems they thought existing Chinese restaurants in Manchester were plagued with. 'We realised that in most restaurants there was either bad food or bad service, and we wanted to open something where the food was really high quality and had good, friendly customer service.' The sisters were also armed with a novel concept; a modern style venue which was a cross between a cocktail bar and a restaurant. But to add an element of authenticity to it they would use and adapt the recipes handed down by their grandmother, setting it apart from the usual Chinatown offering.

Turning the idea into an actual restaurant proved more challenging than initially imagined however. With no suitable sites available they decided they would build one themselves; an undertaking that became the subject of an ITV documentary. Some sound advice from their surveyor eventually led them to their chosen restaurant location, in the Northern Quarter of Manchester. 'At the time the area was quite run down and had virtually no buildings or homes. But there was this one dingy bar rammed with people. We knew that if that bar could attract people, we could start a restaurant there.'

During the building process the sisters made the most of the publicity available to them. They launched a competition for members of the public to name the restaurant, as well as holding auditions for staff in a special 'Asia Babe' contest at local clubs.

The restaurant opened to a rapturous welcome and has continued to build on its own success. Since launching the restaurant the sisters have also received a great deal of press coverage as a result of Helen's book, also entitled *Sweet Mandarin*. The book tells the story of the Tses and their mother and grandmother's life stories.

We're now looking at taking Sweet Mandarin into the supermarkets when we launch our range of sauces. Our long-term plan is to make it a multiplatform brand.'

FRONT OF THE HOUSE – You don't need to accept second rate service staff

Being the daughter of caterers I probably learned how to silver serve even before I knew how to ride a bike. Growing up in Brazil meant that being a waiter is as much of a profession as any other and a lot of training and investment goes into developing people. Typical training for waiting staff can last up to 6 months for level 1.

When I came to the UK I was shocked when my enthusiasm and passion for providing great front of house service were met with a bucket of ice cold water when I worked for hotels and restaurants who seemingly didn't care whether their staff were experienced or well trained, and offered no training to improve the service they offered.

Contrary to popular belief, it takes a lot of training and an eye for detail to be a competent front of the house worker; memory, discretion, flexibility, diplomacy, rapport, technique, communication, posture, elegance, patience, sense of humour are just a few of the skills required in this job. Despite the many media complaints about the poor quality of waiting staff, there is still not enough industry recognition about the importance of providing training.

This has slowly begun to change.

Many UK colleges offer training in hospitality, but those who take these courses rarely stay in front of house positions as they quickly move up to management. For those who think about becoming waiting professionals, the cost in time and money for a college course is often not practical. For those in temporary waiting roles, investing in costly training does not pay off as no employer enforces the need for training.

Tired of this lack of respect for this industry I set up Access Academy, a training consultancy that bridges the gap between the common no-training practice and professional training. It gives trainees an insight into the world of catering and hospitality, so when they go to work they can perform the basic requirements for delivering a good service with confidence.

My dream is that in the future every single venue, restaurant, caterer, hotel and agency will adopt some level of training and no one will be allowed to serve food or drink without training, leading to a better hospitality experience all round.

For more information on how to improve your staff's performance go to **www.accessacademy.org.uk**

1

Before you start

Making it Happen

Once you have opened the doors of your pub, café or restaurant your life will never be the same again.

Your success will rest on your passion for the industry, your ability to achieve high standards, your business acumen and leadership skills. It's a lot to deliver, especially if it's your first venture, so be realistic about your strengths and be prepared to ask for help. Here are four areas to consider:

Understand Your Market

Think about what you offer, the number of customers you need to attract, where your target market is and how you will reach them before choosing your location. Whether you're planning value dining or fine dining, traditional favourites or something more exotic the key is delivering an offer that the local market is looking for. Don't expect your customers to find you, start marketing your business as soon as you can and review your activity so you understand what works best for you.

Maintain High Standards

It's the nature of the industry that a bad experience in your establishment will be talked about more than a good one. Make sure that you set and maintain high standards throughout your business. Whichever end of the market you are operating in there is no excuse for a dirty glass, an unfriendly barman or no loo roll.

Working Partnerships

Opting to work with a pubco partner could be an attractive option. You may think that your location is the key to your success, but many people find the extra support offered through a pubco relationship is vital to their continued achievement. Pubco partners such as Punch can provide additional support like a dedicated business consultant, tailored training programmes and a landlord who has a vested interest in helping you succeed.

Stay on Plan

To take a pub with a pubco you will need to present a full business plan, Once your doors are open you will be immersed in the day to day running of your pub or restaurant, but don't forget to take time to review your performance and look at the bigger picture. Identifying potential issues early will allow you to address them before they become a problem, and if you're doing better than predicted you may wish to update and accelerate your plans to make the most of your investment.

For more information on forming a relationship with a pubco, contact Punch Taverns on **0844 848 3264** or visit **www.punchtaverns.com**

Who, why, what and where?

Y ou've got as far as deciding you'd like to run a restaurant but there's so much to consider before you even start putting a business plan together or suggesting the idea to friends and family.

   You have to decide whether you're prepared for the long hours and the sacrifices you'll have to make. If you're determined to make your dream of running your own restaurant come true, in this chapter we take you through the first steps to making your dream a reality. From getting experience in other restaurants or advice from entrepreneurs, to choosing your business structure; from identifying the key selling points of your idea to conducting market research. After this chapter, you should have a pretty good idea of your concept, and whether it can work.

In this chapter we'll cover:

- Who's suited to running a restaurant
- The experience you need
- Support networks
- Business partners
- Market conditions
- USPs

- Identifying your customers
- Researching the market
- Testing your concept
- Choosing a location
- Buying a business

➡ WHO AND WHY?

Running a restaurant, much like running any business, can only yield real success if you want it enough. But is there a 'type' of person that is more suited to opening up a restaurant? There are reams of studies, reports and research dissecting the DNA of successful business people. The significance of nationality, ethnicity, gender, age, education, class, experience, wealth, sociopolitical demographics, access to support and finance, and every other remotely explorable contributing factor have been analysed to death.

What conclusions have ever been drawn? None worth listening to, other than, in theory at least, there's not anyone, from any background or any walk of life, that can't successfully start and run their own business. So be assured, whatever your concerns and anxieties: you can do it.

'Doing it' is actually far more representative of the average entrepreneur's make-up than any of the numerous factors detailed above. People who start their own business are the ones who stop talking about their dreams and plans and actually make them happen.

Motivation

So what motivates people to do something as time and energy-consuming as starting a restaurant? It's a hard slog, and a career choice which comes with anti-social working hours, a great deal of physical exertion and above all it's an industry difficult to make your millions in.

For surprisingly few, money is the main motivation. For others, being their own boss is the decision-maker. For most it's to realise a dream, idea or desire to live a life that's more fulfilling, whether that be working closer to their family, in an environment they're more comfortable with or simply the challenge of earning their own income.

 FROM THE EXPERTS:
Simon Kossoff, Carluccio's

'Some of the satisfaction you gain comes from looking after people. I don't do it anymore but I used to stand in the middle of a busy restaurant and feel like I was running a party. That's a fantastic feeling and there are a lot of people who do it for that.'

Restaurateurs are a special breed of entrepreneur. You need a passion for people as well as food in this industry. After all, people eat out as a leisure activity, and your restaurant needs to provide them with an entertaining experience.

Some people enter the restaurant industry from a very young age and work their way up to running their own establishment. Some people give up completely different careers, which have nothing to do with the restaurant trade, because they want to work in a more sociable and entertaining environment. Others, such as those made redundant or those who, for whatever reason, struggle to find employment, turn to running their own businesses because they feel it's their only chance for a successful career. People start their own business for individual and deeply personal reasons. As a result, the measure of success isn't necessarily about how much profit you bring in from each evening's diners – it's about achieving personal goals, and hopefully making a decent living at the same time.

Enthusiasm and motivation aren't all it takes of course, as proved by the number of super-keen people who put every last drop of energy into starting a restaurant only to see them fail within the first year. But if you're really determined to do it, you can't be put off by statistics. Yes, people fail, but many succeed as well, and remember, it's a personal measure. Lots of first-time business people don't succeed in others' eyes but use the experience positively to either start another business or return to employment with a greater sense of fulfilment.

Business is all about balancing risk and unless you ensure you're fully aware and prepared for how running a restaurant will impact on your life, you're increasing your risk. Becoming your own boss and setting up a business is one of the most rewarding, exciting and fulfilling things you can do in life, but it's also one of the most stressful, testing and demanding experiences. It's often said getting married and moving house are the two most stressful events most people take on in life but you could quite easily argue starting a business tops that list.

If you think you're escaping the '9 to 5' or 'the rat race' as often referred to in other business books, think again. Forget the idyllic movie representations of business people enjoying long lunches, days on the golf course or at the beauty spa. Gordon Ramsay is probably the most successful, if not the most famous, restaurateur in the UK. According to the 2008 Sunday Times Rich List he's worth £50m. But when was the last time you saw shots of him on a beach, or enjoying a nice holiday in *Hello!* magazine? He works incredibly hard to maintain that level of success. The pace doesn't slow down just because he 'made it' in the restaurant industry.

For at least the first two to three years, put the holidays on hold and expect to work longer and harder than you are now. Expect to make sacrifices with family and friends who, no matter how much you explain, won't understand why you've turned into an obsessed bore who ruins dinner parties and nights out with rants on the price of asparagus or the worsening quality in cuts of meat. You'll need emotional resilience to cope with feeling isolated from your usual support networks; and will need to find the time to create new ones.

For restaurateurs, the long hours can make it hard to meet new contacts. Sure you'll be mixing with the public, but your chances to get out and meet other business owners are limited during opening hours which are likely to be six or seven days a week. The same goes for holidays. Realistically you can only have them if you can afford and trust full-time staff to open up, close, go to the bank for you, not mess up your supplier relationships and get up in the middle of the night if some idiot sets off your alarm.

TIP

If you're finding all this a bit too daunting then you're probably not ready to start your own restaurant yet. However, if reading this has just got you even more fired up for the challenge, you're halfway there already!

Analysing your skills

While passion and determination are compulsory assets for any entrepreneur, in excess they can be dangerous. Critical skills are important and none more so than when looking at yourself – and that starts now. There are certain skills you simply have to have for your restaurant to even make it past the first year.

Here are a few skills you need to run a restaurant:

- A basic understanding of accounting
- An ability or inclination to sell
- Confidence in negotiation
- A natural inquisition for opportunity
- Decisiveness
- Leadership
- Plenty of initiative
- A firm understanding of the customer experience.

There are heads of industry making billion pound decisions affecting hundreds of thousands of people who'll happily admit their skillsets don't stretch to this complete list. The difference is, they have the resources to surround themselves with an army of consultants and advisors.

That's where the reality of running a small restaurant bites: you're highly unlikely to have that luxury from day one – or even day 356 or 752. Running a small business is a demanding, jack-of-all-trades challenge where you, and only you, will be at the centre of all activity. You can hire an accountant and a manager but you'll the need the skills to read the progress of your business in a blink and that takes certain abilities and a rounded perspective.

It's these abilities that dictate who can run a business and who can't. The upside is that you can teach and equip yourself with the basics. If you want to succeed badly enough, you won't be embarrassed about admitting where you need to go back to school, ask questions and get help. You'll make mistakes, learn from them and move on. Remember, each time you do that and pick up something new the risk of failure decreases and chances of success grow. There's more information on identifying your skills and the importance of training in the chapter *You're Open*.

TIP

Ultimately, if you have the desire, are realistic about what you're letting yourself in for, are willing to learn and get your hands dirty, there's certainly no reason why you can't succeed in running a restaurant.

Experience needed

As mentioned previously, many restaurateurs work their way up in the industry, often starting as waiting staff or commis chefs, even kitchen porters. However, there are plenty of successful restaurant owners that have never served or cooked a dish in their lives.

Iqbal Wahhab, The Cinnamon Club and Roast

'I had never served a single plate in a local curry house let alone cooked anything myself in a professional environment when I was looking for investment for The Cinnamon Club. I also had my accountant do all the numbers talk to the investors because it wasn't my strong point. I soon realised that's not what the investor wants to hear, so I had to get to grips with that side of thing myself. The more I did that, the more encouraging the response was from investors.'

Statistically, there's no evidence that people are more likely to succeed if they've been in business before and the increasing numbers of 'teenpreneurs' making their fortunes fresh out of school proves a lack of experience certainly shouldn't be a barrier.

It's also true you'll learn most from the mistakes you'll inevitably make. Just as you only really learn how to drive after you've passed your test, no amount of experience will prepare you for the many unexpected hazards and pitfalls you'll have to learn how to swerve once you're in the driver's seat.

It'd be foolish to discard the value of experience, however. Regardless of what anyone tells you, banks and investors operate on a purely risk against reward policy and the fact they'd prefer a proven track record in the industry over almost any other factor in an investment proposition should tell you everything you need to know about the importance of experience.

Simon Kossoff, Carluccio's

'When I started 30 years ago, to get into a career in the restaurant business, the expectation was that you'd done your time washing dishes and serving customers. It is still like that a little bit now, but not as much as back then.'

It might not be backed up statistically, but it's instinctive to trust someone with experience to do something better than someone just starting out. If you visit the dentist do you place your trust in the senior member of the practice or the latest recruit fresh out of college? There's no reason why the junior wouldn't have a wider knowledge of the latest practices and be the more skilled operator of course, but he or she would have it all to prove and that's the position you'll find yourself in if you go into the restaurant trade without any experience.

It's also a fair assumption that the more experience you have, the better informed your decisions are. The more pitfalls you know about, the earlier you'll see them and easier it'll be to avoid them. Founder of easyJet and the numerous easyGroup brands, Sir Stelios Haji-Innonou, is known as a risk-taker, and while a supporter of young entrepreneurs, he believes 28 is a better age to start a business than straight from school or university because by then you'll have had time to understand how companies operate and, crucially, make mistakes at someone else's expense.

In essence, this is fairly obvious. However, by the very fact you feel it necessary to pick up this book, it's probably safe to assume you haven't previously started and run your own restaurant, or at least not for a long time. It might be that you have business experience. Maybe you've run a different business in the past or come from an accounting background so feel comfortable in business models and making the books balance, or you're a champion sales or marketing person who thinks you're capable making any business a success.

TIP

The danger comes in assumption. Too many people think because they know how to cook, or host a great dinner party and have a bit of business acumen too, they know what it takes to run a thriving restaurant. Likewise just because you've run the finance function of a blue chip company it doesn't mean you'll understand how to squeeze the best margin out of particular dish on the menu.

Just because you've eaten in a lot of restaurants it doesn't mean you've any idea how to run one. Be careful you don't fall into this trap. For instance, when you ate out last week were you really thinking about what shifts the person serving you was on that week, how much they earned, what percentage of the restaurant's income that was, how much the mark up on the menu was, how many covers ordered that dish, when the next delivery was due or who lets the cleaners in and out at unsociable hours?

It's always different on the other side of the kitchen and no matter how much you think you already know, there will be more to learn. Alan Yau grew up in the restaurant industry and has gone on to have great success with Wagamama and Hakkasan. However, he initially struggled with Wagamama's promise to deliver food quickly in a less formal environment. To get a better understanding of the process of serving fast food he got a job at Burger King to find out how the industry worked and what he could take from it.

Where possible your experience should be relevant to the type of restaurant you want to run. A fast food or café-style restaurant will be run very differently to a gourmet French bistro for example. Experience can help you find quicker solutions when you come across roadblocks but you shouldn't necessarily be put off from opening a restaurant if you've never worked in catering. No matter what it says in the business manuals, if you've set your heart on starting-up and got as far as buying this book, you probably don't want to put your grand plans on hold for years while you complete a hospitality internship.

Gaining the relevant experience

Most people know they should probably get some experience but aren't sure where to fit it in or even how to get the experience. If you're working full-time it's often unrealistic to expect you to get a job in a kitchen during the evenings, especially if you've got family commitments. Likewise, once you've stopped working and sacrificed the security of a salary, getting a job in a restaurant for the sake of picking up some experience can use up valuable planning time.

There's no one answer that'll work for everyone. For some people, getting a job in a restaurant at the weekend while you serve out your notice of employment is the obvious solution; for others it's a case of dedicating a period of your pre-start-up or 'research' time to getting some inside information.

IN MY EXPERIENCE:

Geetie Singh, The Duke of Cambridge

'My first steps were to talk to people who had set up businesses, and as well as being told I needed a good business plan, I was told I needed more experience. So I thought about the areas of expertise I was lacking in and got jobs in those environments. I worked with the Pelican Group, which owned Café Rouge, to learn the formality of tight systems with strict rules in order to monitor margins and profits. I got a job in a very fine restaurant to learn about their wine list and formal dining. I also got a job in a wholefood shop so I could learn about organic produce and sustainable sourcing.'

It might seem awkward to apply for a job you're not committed to or perhaps even over-qualified for, and it's not beyond comprehension you'll be asked about this. Here you have a straight choice to come clean or lie. The choice is yours but you'll be surprised how many owner-managers will understand your situation and welcome the help of someone who's keen to learn, especially if you're able to offer them your services for free.

If you're really unable to commit a period of time to getting experience, ask a restaurateur if you can shadow them for a typical day in the life of the business – or at the very least ask if you can buy them a meal or a drink in exchange for them imparting their wisdom.

It makes sense to do some work in the type of restaurant you're planning to open, or observe it from an inside point of view. Talk to restaurateurs that run similar operations to the one you're planning. As long as they're in a completely different area and your business won't open in competition to theirs, you may find they're willing to let you gain a little experience or observe how they run their kitchen.

Making these initial contacts might feel awkward and scary, especially if you're not accustomed to the world of business networking, but just remember, all the people you approach were once in your position. If you get a no – polite or otherwise – just brush it off and move on to someone else.

Support networks

The first support network you'll need is your family and friends, regardless of whether they're directly involved or not. No matter how hard you attempt to make sure it doesn't, starting and running a business will impact on your family, so it's essential you prepare them for what's ahead. If your family (spouse, children, parents) aren't on board with you 100%, at some point you, your business, and/or your family will bear the consequences.

New businesses require a tremendous amount of time and nurturing to develop and become successful; time that is taken from elsewhere, often from the family. Unless you're starting a 'family' business where all members are participants, someone will inevitably feel left out, or neglected. Our family members don't always share the same dream as we do. Their priorities may be something far from business success.

To make sure your family doesn't suffer due to your own ambitions, before you pursue your dream business, sit down with them and discuss the following:

- Will the business venture take away from quality time spent with family members? If so, how much is acceptable to all involved?
- Will the new business be initially funded or supported using family monies? If so, will this put a financial strain on the family?
- Do all family members agree this is a potentially successful business idea?
- Do all family members realise that most new businesses do not succeed?
- If the business is not showing signs of becoming successful, what operational time period will the family tolerate before the business is considered a failure and should be sold or closed down?
- If the new business fails, what is the alternative plan for income?

Some of the questions listed above may not have obvious answers until the business has started up and operated for some period of time. Since circumstances may vary regularly with new business, plan to review this list with your family about every six months to see what situations may have changed.

Your family needs to be in total support of your new business idea, or somewhere and at some point, somebody will suffer. Consider whether your 'big idea' is worth the possibility of distancing yourself from your loved ones. Business owners with complete family support stand a much greater chance of success. Talk to your family and trust in their opinion.

IN MY EXPERIENCE:
Shevonne Bennett, Brown Sugar

'I didn't tell my family what I was planning straight away because I was scared of the backlash. I had a HR degree and a Masters in that field and was working in that sector at the time. But I knew the 9 to 5 lifestyle wasn't for me, so I started working on my business plan while I was in full-time employment.'

Other entrepreneurs

The reason we asked some of the leading names in the restaurant industry to contribute to this book is that there's simply no better place to get advice than from those that have, as the saying goes, 'been there, done it and got the t-shirt'.

Entrepreneurs trust other entrepreneurs more than anyone else and naturally form support networks that might at first appear cliquey but are almost always actually born simply out of a shared understanding of each other's fairly unique lives.

Like all relationships you'll find that with support networks you'll get out what you put in. Networking comes naturally to some people; it fills others with dread. If you're the first sort of person, you're probably already aware of the value of getting out and meeting others. In business you can't know too many people or have enough 'friends' to call on to get you out of a mess. If you're the second type of person, you're going to have to be brave and bite the bullet. Get yourself to a business networking event, have a glass of wine and simply chat to people about what you're doing.

> ### ✦ TIP
> Events like Startups Live, which you can find more details on at www.startupslive.co.uk, will give you the opportunity to meet hundreds of other budding entrepreneurs and new business owners, some of whom will know the answers to the questions you're struggling to find answers to. The likelihood is it won't be half as scary as you make it out to be in your mind and, remember, most people have been, or still are, in the same boat as you.

Networking is also a great way of picking up recommendations. Most people recommend people they use – whether good or bad – so don't swallow their advice blindly, but knowing an accountant or lawyer who's experienced in your sector or knowledgeable in the area is a far more valuable lead than your standard Google search.

Don't confine your networking to physical events, either. Social networking is growing beyond the fun and games of Facebook and MySpace into a serious business tool and with sites such as LinkedIn, Smarta.com, BT Tradespace and Startups.co.uk you can interact with other entrepreneurs and business advisors – and, of course, while it lacks face-to-face personal touch it's far less scary!

Also see what business bodies and lobby groups are out there both for small business and restaurateurs. The Federation of Small Businesses, Forum of Private Businesses and British Chambers of Commerce are all recognised lobby and small business groups who aim to represent, champion and advise small businesses of all industries. However, there are also plenty of more restaurant specific organisations such as the Restaurant Association and the British Hospitality Association (BHA).

As well as at Startups.co.uk, the government's official support service Business Link can provide you with practical advice, and it's worth reading up as much as you can about the various aspects of starting a business you're most concerned about. There's a wealth of information out there so take advantage of it.

Business mentoring

Finally, think about getting a mentor. The government is set to announce a national mentoring service and there are several organisations who provide matching services such as the Prince's Trust, Horsesmouth and the Rockstar Group.

You don't have to follow this route, though. You also don't need a high profile celebrity entrepreneur mentor. Someone who's done what you wish to do should be your number one criteria. An experienced entrepreneur who you can turn to once every month or so to test out ideas on, and get advice from, will prove just, if not more, valuable.

Don't be scared to approach someone you don't know. Many entrepreneurs feel a responsibility to encourage and help others and will be only too willing to help. If they're not it'll almost certainly be because they're simply too busy (either running their own businesses still or possibly helping someone else). If that's the case, ask someone else. You'll soon get used to moving on quickly and without a grudge when met with the word 'no'! There's a whole section on Startups.co.uk on how to find, approach and deal with a business mentor. The website will also point you in the right direction to getting a mentor on board for your own business.

The more support you actively surround yourself with, the less likely you'll feel like you're in this on your own. For all the highs running your own restaurant will bring, there will be down times too and you'll soon find your family, friends and knowledgeable contacts can be worth their weight in gold.

Lobby groups and support organisations

The Federation of Small Businesses (FSB)	www.fsb.org.uk
The Forum of Private Business (FPB)	www.fpb.org
The British Chambers of Commerce (BCC)	www.britishchambers.org.uk
Restaurant Association (part of the BHA)	www.bha.org.uk
Business Link	www.businesslink.gov.uk
Regional Development Agencies	www.englandsrdas.com

Going into business with partners/friends

Restaurants are a popular type of business to go into with family or even friends. After years of living separate working lives, couples often see a restaurant as a way of spending more time together. Likewise, who better to trust sharing such an enormous financial and emotional challenge with than your closest friends?

It's easy to see why, idealistically at least, it appeals. When you consider how much of our waking lives we spend earning money to enjoy in comparatively small spaces of time with the people that mean most to us, combining the two to get the best of both worlds is a compelling argument. What's more, it can work brilliantly. The attributes for a healthy relationship – trust, honesty, the ability to listen, understanding, the unity of or tolerance of shared or different interests – translate well into business.

FROM THE EXPERTS:
Simon Kossoff, Carluccio's

'I was working with the Radio Café that had sites including Leicester Square and Birmingham and it was around that time I met Antonio and Pricilla Carluccio. Pricilla had already had the idea for an all-day café with a shop in it. She wanted it to be a brand that could roll out, and had a very clear idea about what it would be like, but didn't have the skills in her team to develop the idea, get funding or find sites etc. So we came together along with two of my ex-colleagues to build it.'

Shared understanding about responsibility is the key to making a business started with friends or family work. It's essential to be sure that aside from your personal relationships, there's a business case for working together. Ideally your skillsets should complement each other so the restaurant benefits from supporting two people – if it's unlikely you'd otherwise recruit this person alarm bells should be ringing.

If your decision to work together does make business sense, there's no reason you shouldn't continue: just be aware of the consequences. If the business doesn't work out then relationships could turn sour and the trauma of losing a business could be doubled by also losing an otherwise lifelong friend or partner. Is the sharing of your finances and knowledge worth the sacrifice? Ultimately it's your call, but be wary of rushing into something you could regret and agree how you'll communicate inevitable frustrations with each other to keep the relationship healthy.

If your business partner is more of an associate than a friend, you need to be clear in your mind that you trust and like this person sufficiently to share such an epic journey with them. It's likely you'll be working intensively with them for a number of years so you'll clearly need to get on.

IN MY EXPERIENCE:

Geetie Singh, The Duke of Cambridge

'While trying to write a business plan I realised I needed a business partner to help me through that stage and I went through a couple. One was a total disaster, but then I found Esther [Boulton], who was very academically minded and good at the writing side of things. I was the kind of front woman and she did all the back work. It worked really well. We would go to meetings and she'd take lots of notes while I did all the talking. We were a neat little team.'

Aside from having the skills you don't have and vice versa, look for a partner with whom you have a natural business chemistry; someone who can enthuse you and whom you can inspire. Good partnerships, from business to sport and even entertainment, combine characters who together can create a greater sum total than their individual efforts and that's what you should aspire to build.

 TIP

Don't be tempted to go into business with someone simply because they've financial backing and you haven't, or because they've the great contacts you need. If a partnership doesn't have a natural foundation it won't work.

You'll need to balance reward, responsibility and risk. Make sure you're clear what your goals are for the business on a shared and personal level, what you want in the short, medium and long-term, be clear what your respective roles are and ensure you're each staking the same degree of risk. And, simple as it sounds, make sure you're happy and comfortable and have clear lines of communication for it to stay that way.

However, with all partnerships, expect the unexpected. Two out of three marriages end in divorce and while that shouldn't dissuade you from entering into a commitment with someone, similarly it should be enough of a warning to get a legally binding shareholder agreements drawn up if you decided to go into business with someone. This should cover what happens to the business and shares if any combination of unthinkable outcomes occur including, as morbid as it might seem, either of your deaths. Type 'shareholder agreement' into Google and you'll find plenty of companies willing to do this for you for as little as £50. You can also have your solicitor draw something up.

Market conditions

It's likely you've heard a lot about the current economic downturn. You may have even felt the impact on your mortgage repayments, shopping bill or at the petrol station. There's no denying that economically it's a difficult time and unlike previous dips, a quick resolution doesn't appear forthcoming.

Banks have cut lending options and it's certainly a tougher climate in which to raise funds for a business than a few short years ago. This, of course, also impacts on what people have to spend, and leisure activities such as eating out suddenly become less affordable for a lot of people. But essentially, there's never a bad time to start a good business, so don't let market conditions put you off: just make sure you plan even harder to get your offering spot on.

The stats to get your teeth into

An impressive five new restaurants opened every day in the UK during 2007, according to research by catering industry organisation Startupsplus.

In total that makes 1,803 restaurants, which exceeded the number of takeaways by about 100, suggesting the UK is moving away from a culture of take-home meals in favour of a full restaurant dining experience. Among all these new restaurants, the most popular type to open served ethnic speciality food. Indian and Chinese restaurants accounted for a quarter of all new restaurants. In total, out of all the restaurants opened in 2007, 40% of them served ethnic food ranging from Persian to Korean.

However before you get too excited about the fact that nearly 2,000 new restaurants opened in 2007, bear in mind that in 2003 the UK had 25,964 restaurants. However, in 2006 the number stood at 26,629. That's growth of less than a thousand, meaning there area a great deal of closures too.

Five new restaurants a day equates to a lot of new places to eat out, but are there enough new restaurant diners to fill the tables? The lack of overall growth in the total number of outlets open suggests maybe there aren't, but according to the British Hospitality Association (BHA), the number of meals eaten out in the UK has been growing at an average rate of 2% since 2006. That's more than double the rate of growth over the previous five years. Surprisingly this 2% growth has taken into account a drop in the popularity of fast-food eateries, which are widely being shunned in favour of more a more formal dining experience.

However, it seems all this choice in where to eat out is keeping menu inflation low. The average price paid per head in a restaurant in 2007 was £10.42. This figure obviously includes cheaper fast food eateries. The thing to note is the 2007 figure is only 0.4% higher than the year before. However, rising food prices may soon take its toll, and many restaurateurs will be forced to put prices up to maintain a healthy margin.

So what's this industry worth? The BHA estimates the number of meals served in the UK in 2007 to be worth £750m. While there's a few words of caution to be taken from these statistics, there's also the suggestion that it's a big enough pie for you to have a small slice.

WHAT/WHERE?

Your big idea – USPs

You'll probably already know what type of restaurant you want to open. Indeed, when you first stumbled upon the idea of getting into the business, you were almost certainly thinking of running a certain type of establishment.

For many of you it'll be as simple as wanting to run the type of restaurant you've always enjoyed eating in. For others among you, a restaurant will represent an opportunity to spend your working day embracing a hobby, such as entertaining people, playing host or indulging in a passion for great food and wine. The more opportunistic and entrepreneurial among you will have spotted a trend or gap in the market for a certain type of restaurant however.

 IN MY EXPERIENCE:

Geetie Singh, The Duke of Cambridge

'Right from the beginning, the moment I decided to open my own place, I knew exactly what I wanted. I had been a restaurateur for a long time so knew what I wanted from my own. There was the clear concept of what it would look and feel like, and running side-by-side with that were the sustainable values behind the business.'

Picking the type of cuisine you'll serve is only half the challenge. Next you'll need to explore the specifics of the type of dining experience you want and start sculpting exactly what your offering to the market will be. It's not enough to say you want to start an Italian restaurant. Caluccio's offers Italian-style food, but in a very different environment to your average family-run pizzeria. You need to establish your place in the market. Will you be catering for high-end diners or casual shoppers wanting a quick, cheap bite to eat?

Start by making a list of what will make your restaurant unique. Your USPs (Unique Selling Points) will define how your place is different from the competition and will slowly build its identity and brand.

 TIP

There are sure to be many more USPs to differentiate your business. Don't try and add them for the sake of it, but ensure your business is clearly defined from what's already out there and that you have a firm idea of what makes your offering special.

For example, Simon Woodroffe created a whole new kind of dining experience in the UK by introducing a conveyor belt on which to serve food. There were plenty of sushi restaurants around, but Simon opened one with a completely unique proposition. Likewise combining the deli-style retail section and dining area gave Carluccio's a fresh take on the theme of Italian restaurant.

When drawing up your USPs, consider the following suggestions to differentiate your offering:

- Superior customer service
- No frills
- A more niche or premium selection of food
- Budget offering
- Child-friendly atmosphere
- Faster or quicker dining experience
- Luxury dining experience
- Combination of food and entertainment – live music etc.
- Ethically sourced
- Environmentally friendly.

IN MY EXPERIENCE:
Lisa Tse, Sweet Mandarin

'When we came back to Manchester after a family holiday to Hong Kong we realised that a lot of restaurants either had bad food or bad service. We wanted to open a restaurant with high quality food and good friendly customer service. The concept was also quite unique because it was a cross between a cocktail bar and a Chinese restaurant. Added to that, we were using my grandmother, and mother's, recipes so it was different to what they were serving in Chinatown.'

Who are your customers?

Once you've a clear idea of what type of food your restaurant will serve and what its USPs are, you need to define who your customers will be. Without doing this you won't be able to properly plot the viability of your business in a business plan.

To assess if your restaurant will succeed as a business you'll need to prove there are enough people in the area you're based in who want to dine out for the price you're serving food for. For some restaurants reliant on tourism, or affected by seasonal peaks and troughs, this can be a complicated process and will involve looking at visitor levels as well as regional populations; calculating varying incomes against monthly and annual overheads.

Don't fall for the mistake of convincing yourself that just because you love the idea, then others will. Too many people skip the process believing 'if you build it, they will come'. It's a saying built in Hollywood not the real world, where the reality is people can't come if they don't exist . . . or they can't afford your prices . . . or there's a restaurant doing the same thing two doors down.

Unfortunately there are plenty of great sounding 'ideas' that simply aren't viable. Banks will expect to see evidence of an existing customer base and so should you if you're using your own money or, quite simply, you want the business to have a chance of working.

Before you can explore whether your customer exists in sufficient numbers you need to establish exactly who you're looking for. There are standard demographic outlines of consumers you should use.

Social grade	Social status	Occupation	Annual earnings estimate
A	upper middle class	higher managerial, administrative or professional	£50k +
B	middle class	intermediate managerial, administrative or professional	£35–£50k
C1	lower middle class	supervisory or clerical, junior managerial, administrative or professional	£25–£35k
C2	skilled working class	skilled manual workers	£15–£25k
D	working class	semi and unskilled manual workers	£7–£15k
E	those at lowest level of subsistence	state pensioners or widows (no other earner), casual or lowest grade workers	£5–£7k

You essentially want to know what the profile of your target customer is: are they male or female? How old are they? What's their disposable income? What brands do they also consume? How much would they spend with you and how frequently?

FROM THE EXPERTS:
Iqbal Wahhab, The Cinnamon Club and Roast

'I had a very clear idea in my mind of what I wanted to achieve. I wanted an Indian restaurant that wasn't constrained by the parameters that existing restaurant owners thought fine dining should be about. Other top-end Indian restaurants were charging the same prices as top-end French restaurants without changing the menu regularly or showing the same interest level in the provenance of ingredients.'

Research the market

Now you know what type of restaurant you want to start and who you'd ideally like your prime customers to be, you need to know if those people actually exist. Not only must they exist, they must exist where you can find and afford premises.

One of the best places to start is by getting hold of a copy of your area's latest census, either online at www.ons.gov.uk/census or from your local library. Even better, get hold of censuses for several areas you could feasibly operate in so you can make direct comparisons – even if you're stuck on one location, having stats proving its suitability can make a compelling case to the bank so is still worth doing.

The census will give you all sorts of information such as the population of the area; percentage of home ownership; percentage of people economically active (employed); the percentage of those retired. The good thing about a census is it uses the same questions for all areas so it's easy to compare the results of one region to another. Additionally there are several websites available that provide regional demographic information, such as www.upmystreet.com.

Consult restaurant statistics released by the British Hospitality Associations and similar groups to identify trends in the type of restaurant you're looking to start and look for breakdowns by region. Business Link and The British Library can also give you access to market reports and data that would cost thousands of pounds to buy copies of yourself.

> **Useful market research contacts**
>
> British Hospitality Association: www.bha.org.uk
> Business Link: www.businesslink.gov.uk
> The British Library: www.bl.uk

Research companies and DIY surveys

Carry out your own research with the public as well. Take to the streets and carry out surveys and questionnaires exploring anything that can prove your case that a market for your restaurant exists. Ask respondents how often they would eat out a month in a restaurant of your type and price, and how far they'd come for food served with your USP. Asking personal questions such as people's income or age is likely to put them off taking part, so instead ask them to tick ranges which will fit with the demographic research you've unearthed and have identified as your target customer. The more people you interview within these ranges, the more powerful your research will be.

> **DIY market research**
>
> Questions to ask members of the public in your chosen location:
>
> - How often do you eat out – hardly ever, once or twice a month, once or twice a week, more than twice a week?
> - How old are you – under 18, 18–24, 25–34, 35–50, 50+?
> - What's your wage bracket – under £15,000, £15–£20,000, £20–£30,000, £30–£50,000, £50–£100,000, £100,000+?
> - Do you normally visit restaurants for – entertainment, convenience, other?
> - Would you welcome a restaurant serving [enter your type of food here]
> - What do think a reasonable cost for a starter/main meal/dessert is for a restaurant in this area?

There are professional research companies that you can hire to carry out feasibility studies. For most of you their services will be out of your price range and be wary of companies who claim to do this for comparatively low rates as it's likely they'll merely accumulate information already in the public domain that you could do for yourself.

Well carried-out professional research can prove worth the investment however, especially if you're seeking substantial finance. If you pursue this route, be clear about exactly what you're looking to achieve and perhaps even research what investors want first and find out how you can meet their expectations. However, be careful what you spend. While some investors will be impressed by professional research, others will question your business acumen if you've spent a considerable slice of your start-up capital just proving a market exists.

TIP

Try the Research Buyers Guide when looking for reputable sources for market research. www.rbg.org.uk has a fully searchable directory of market research providers.

Competition

Competition tends to come in two forms: directly from other restaurants in your area, and indirectly from other ways customers can spend money they'd otherwise spend with you. Direct competition is relatively simple to research and observe, but indirect competition is subject to constant change, market forces and trends. For instance, the retail industry has enjoyed tremendous growth over the last couple of decades as increasing numbers of people spend more of their income on eating out. However, in times of economic difficulty people will go for cheaper options, perhaps buying luxury food from shops rather than paying an extra £30 to have it cooked for them and served.

Competition isn't always a negative however, and can be seen as collaborative. Restaurants and estate agents have prospered for years by clustering together and the successful rise of retail parks full of rival retailers is proof it can often pay to be located alongside competitors. Indeed, a highly successful restaurant in an area could suggest there's room for another, especially if customers are frustrated at not being able to get a table in the only good restaurant in the area. Competition then should be seen as an opportunity to prove the case for your business as well as a reason for disproving it.

You should cross reference the number of competitors in your area, and their USPs, with your demographics in order to establish if there's room for another business. It could be that on reflection you identify a new USP that would give you a better chance of securing market share – and that's perfectly healthy.

Competitors should also provide a way of benchmarking your proposition and pricing. Visit them, take in the dining experience, where possible speak to customers to get a feel for their reputation and try to identify as many places as possible where you can score an advantage.

TIP

If you're feeling especially brave, go and speak to the owners. Be honest and say you're thinking of starting a restaurant in the area, ask them for tips and advice. You'll find many are surprisingly helpful and even with the ones that aren't, you won't be any worse off, and you'll know more about the kind of people you're up against.

How to test your concept

Take every opportunity you can to test your concept. It's likely you'll still be tweaking it a year into opening, but by then you'll have all the overheads, time constraints and running responsibilities to deal with, so take every chance you get while researching and starting-up to test, test and then test again.

Visit markets, fairs, fêtes, car boot sales – anywhere you've a captive audience to sample your food – and get feedback. To test if people like what you have to offer, give some away in exchange for honest feedback – and that doesn't mean to friends and family whose opinion is always biased no matter how much they insist they're being truthful. For any concept testing you do, make sure you record the results. It's all good for tweaking your model and also compelling evidence to use in your business plan and when pitching for finance or even for PR.

The founders of Innocent Drinks constantly refer to the day they tested a selection of initial smoothie recipes out on visitors to a jazz festival, asking people to place their empty cups in either a 'yes' or 'no' bin under the banner 'Should we quit our jobs to make these smoothies full-time?'. The more feedback you can get, the closer you'll be to serving food people actually want once you're open and hopefully you'll be building customer and brand awareness along the way.

Choosing the right location

We'll concentrate on choosing your location in far more detail in *Finding Property*, but it is something you have to consider carefully during the planning stage. Considering your location isn't just about picking an area to set up your restaurant in. You need to consider everything from whether you'll be located on a high street or a shopping centre, right down to what side of the road you're positioned on.

By now you should have proven there's a significant volume of customers in the town or city you're looking to open your shop, but that's only half the battle. Unfortunately, even a great restaurant with fantastic food at a great price won't guarantee sufficient visitors unless you find a location that makes it convenient to get people through the doors.

The local council might be able to provide local footfall figures, detailing walk-through populations by street. Market research companies will also sell you this, but it's something you can measure yourself. If you do, be careful to take samples at different times of the day taking into account traditional periods of influential activity such as rush hours, lunch times, after pub closing etc.

It's also worth speaking to your local council or regional development agency to see if there are any incentives, grants or tax breaks for opening in a certain area – or even relocating to a different city. It might not be what you had planned, but free rent and a support grant could make all the difference to your business' survival.

Buying an existing business

You don't have to start from scratch and restaurants are one of the most popular businesses to buy. There are many reasons to buy instead of setting up. As well as premises, you'll be acquiring a ready-made proposition and customer base. It'll certainly take less time than starting up yourself and if you buy a healthy, profitable restaurant it'll almost certainly be cheaper too as it's more likely to survive than a new business.

The challenge is finding a business to buy that is 'healthy and profitable' and doesn't just have the potential to be, or worse still, has no chance of fulfilling its potential. What you won't ever see is a sales blurb telling you this. It'll be up to you to distinguish what's worth buying and what's not and it's a notorious minefield.

Some of the world's top entrepreneurs and restaurateurs have been lured by a bargain convinced they'll be able to sprinkle their magic dust and turn a profit – but have failed. For the first-time buyer, buying a business is riddled with risk but then so is starting up. If you decide to buy a restaurant, do as much homework as you can in a bid to limit that risk. Time is often limited but the more information you can find out about exactly what you're buying, the better informed you'll be about the price you should be paying and exactly what you're letting yourself in for.

Do your research

Make sure you speak to people. Ideally you'll want to speak to the sellers. If you're buying direct this won't be a problem but be wary of sellers who are reluctant to divulge too much information or open up the books; you can be sure there's a reason why. Be careful too if you're buying through an agency which is reluctant for you to speak to the seller directly. A good seller will be open about their reasons for selling, although it's fair to assume someone will be more forthcoming about wanting to retire or move away than dwindling sales – but you should be able to see this from their books.

Speaking to the owners will also help you establish if it's worth paying for 'goodwill', where you pay a premium in exchange for existing client contacts and customer information and the reputation the place has built up within the community. Speak to customers (if the sellers are happy for you to do this, it's a good sign); customers visiting competitors (ask them why they're not eating at the place you're looking to buy and what would make them change their mind); and chat to suppliers to establish how relationships have been left and to suss out any bad debts.

Make sure you speak to staff as well. If you take over you'll be expected to honour their contracts under the TUPE regulations but just as importantly, they'll know the business better than you will. Keeping them on board, at least until you've found your feet, is likely to make sense and be good for continuity.

 TIP

Get an accountant involved. They'll be able to check the books for anything concerning or unscrupulous and will also advise you on the most tax efficient way to structure the purchase.

Once you've made a purchase, it's likely you'll still want to stamp your authority on the business. Certainly you'll need to be just as clear in your offering as if you were starting from fresh. The rest of this book is about starting a restaurant, but all the principles covered are just as relevant to the first time restaurateur who's acquired a business as has started their own.

Things to remember:

- It's too much hard work to start if you're not fully committed to seeing it through. Know what you're getting into before you start.

- If you don't have enough experience, get some before you open.

- Talk it through with friends and family. They may still offer support even if they're not convinced by the idea.

- If you can't do it alone, think long and hard about the type of person you want as a partner.

- Identify a USP from the very beginning.

- Do your research, and make it thorough.

- Know your competition inside out.

- Don't rule out the possibility of buying and adding to an existing business.

B usiness plans feature first in this chapter because it's absolutely imperative that you perfect your business plan before you start pitching for investment, looking for premises or deciding on your branding. It needs to outline how your restaurant is going to be financially viable, how you plan to grow it and include a really accurate assessment of what you'll spend to get it off the ground.

We lay out all the information a good plan needs to include and how this will help you not only to secure funding for your venture but also equip you with a clear vision of how you are going to run your restaurant both now and in the future. By including details of your pricing strategy, your expenses, your predicted revenue and financial records you'll be left with a business plan which will be a useful tool you can adapt and refer to as your business plans progress.

In this chapter we'll cover:

- Writing your business plan
- Setting prices
- Revenue forecasts
- Financial sheets
- Budgeting

➡ BUSINESS PLAN

Don't be put off by writing a business plan. It's not difficult and if you do it properly it won't be tedious either. It should be a labour of love and every bit as exciting as the initial idea-generating enthusiasm that led you to pick up this book. Writing a business plan should further feed that enthusiasm. Why? Because by the end of the process you should feel you're able to transcend from idea to an actual restaurant. What's more you should have a document for others to believe you too.

IN MY EXPERIENCE:
Shevonne Bennett, Brown Sugar

'I started working on my business plan while I was working full-time, and I set myself goals to achieve – a month, three months, a year. I really felt that if I put my mind to it, I could get the formula right so I started going to marketing and business seminars, and getting friends and acquaintances to review my business plan. I consulted a lot of people in the industry – chefs, restaurateurs – and did a lot of networking. It's surprising how small a community it is when you start looking.'

Certainly, there's no avoiding writing a business plan; and the more you embrace it the more you're likely to actually find it a meaningful and useful process than merely a way of appeasing the bank. A good business plan will give you something to constantly refer back to when making tough decisions and strategy calls, and should be a working document you update as the business progresses.

Before you start putting a plan together, try and get hold of some examples from the internet or even ask your bank what sort of document they expect to see. Don't worry too much about the design and layout of a business plan at this stage, though. Much like CVs, people often obsess unnecessarily about the supposed best format, structure, length and layout when what's far more important is that the document contains all the necessary information and is easy to understand.

What to include

Start by identifying and gathering the basic information you'll need. A standard business plan should outline the following:

- What your restaurant will do
- Who your customers will be
- Why people will eat in your restaurant
- Evidence this market exists and its potential
- Evidence of why your business will survive when others don't; analysis of the competition
- Who you are and why you're going into business
- Why you believe you've got the skills and expertise to run a restaurant; your qualifications and experience
- Details of any other directors or key management
- How you will fund the setting up of the business
- How you will repay any money you borrow
- What your ongoing costs and overheads will be
- Sales and revenue forecasts for the first 12 months of business
- Details of suppliers and contracts
- Your goals for the first 12 months and then beyond that

That might sound fairly exhaustive, but it should be. Your business plan should present a watertight argument of why and how your restaurant will work. If it's not, then you should be asking yourself if it's still such a great idea.

Be honest and don't exaggerate revenues and underplay overheads in order to make the plan work. Bank managers will have seen thousands of applications in their time and will see straight through it – and, of course, you'll be kidding yourself and invalidating your business plan as a useful document. If anything, veer on the side of caution.

Many entrepreneurs have said, with the benefit of hindsight, when planning a business you should halve the income you anticipate and double the expenses you expect to pay – any discrepancy in your favour will be a bonus. Others insist

> ### ⭐ TIP
> Use your business plan to prove to yourself that your venture can survive and prosper, not just as a tool to accessing finance.

they would never have secured the funding they needed without a few white lies and that whatever you ask for, the bank will give you 20% less. Ultimately it's your call, but remember your business plan should plot your progress and skewing it for any purpose limits how much it can help you.

Keep it simple and don't write reams – an overly long verbose plan will irritate more than it impresses and investors will be far more concerned with being able to access concise key information than they will your poetic flair or pretty paper; it's a business plan not a Year 9 school project. Where appropriate use bullet points and break up the text; bitesize chunks of information are far easier to absorb. Don't leave anything out but keep it brief; people can always contact you if they need to know more.

➡ SETTING YOUR PRICES

Before you can plan anything; make any forecasts; plot any projections or arrive at a principle sum you'll need to borrow to start your restaurant, you need to think about roughly how much money you can make from the food and drink you intend to serve. As it's difficult to tell exactly how much you'll serve, it's safer to start by looking at how much profit you can make per dish sold. To do this, you'll need to start setting prices.

Calculating prices

Exactly how much you intend to sell individual dishes for might seem like minutiae that can wait until later when you've 'big vision' considerations such as securing a bank loan, finding premises and creating a brand etc. However, it's actually a much bigger factor in deciding whether your business will work than any of those, and as such needs to be at the forefront of your planning. You can't possibly know how feasible a business is without being clear about the fundamentals of any catering operation: how much money you make per plate.

There are two key elements of deciding how much your prices will be:

1. The costs of ingredients
2. Your operational expenses

The cost of ingredients should include any associated cost in the development or acquiring process such as packaging and delivery etc. Operational expense incorporates all your overheads, rent, staff wages, marketing, technology etc.

The sum of the two costs subtracted from the price you set will, in theory, be the profit you generate – although, of course, there are many outside influences that have the potential to impact on your bottom line.

You'll need to begin by ensuring you know exactly how much your food costs to the point where it ends up on a customer's bill. You'll also need to establish the running costs of your business. You probably don't know all of them at the moment so make estimations and keep tweaking and adjusting the calculation when you know more.

Know your figures

When the likes of Peter Jones and Duncan Bannatyne berate budding entrepreneurs on *Dragons' Den* for not 'knowing their figures' this is exactly what they're talking about – and they're right as well. For your restaurant to succeed as a business, which is exactly what it is, you'll need to know at all points what any dish or drink you sell costs you to buy and how much you make when you sell it. If you can't do this you cease to be running a business, whose aim, remember, over and above all the lifestyle benefits it brings you, is to make money. It's that profit that will pay your salaries, mortgage and holidays, and what the bank manager or an investor needs to be confident of if they are to lend you money.

Developing a pricing strategy

Unfortunately knowing what a dish costs you and the percentage of profit you'd like to make is rarely all it takes to make your restaurant's proposition viable. The missing key consideration in this equation is a customer base that wants to buy at this golden figure you've got sitting on your calculator. To a certain extent your prices will be determined by the quality of ingredients used, and the level of service or experience you offer your customers when they dine with you.

If you do decide to price below your competitors you'll need to work on keeping your overheads rock bottom. In times of troubled economic climates, diners might decide not to eat as much. However, for those that still want to eat out, tighter purse strings may attract them to a cheaper menu.

One way of pricing your menu for maximum profit is to have a higher

> **TIP**
> While on the subject of pricing, it's important to remember your obligations under the Price Marking Order 1979, which states you must display your prices clearly at the entrance to the restaurant.

profit margin on certain items such as wine, drinks, desserts etc. That way if you don't make as much profit on items such as main dishes, this can be offset by the sale of other items. The average food cost percentage restaurateurs use is somewhere between 20%–40%.

IN MY EXPERIENCE:
Geetie Singh, The Duke of Cambridge

'My business partner Esther came up with a really comprehensive business plan. I hadn't even written an essay from what I could remember and I found that very intimidating. The plan was beautiful, with pictures of interiors and how it would all look. I also got all our figures from other restaurateurs I knew and had worked with. Everyone was willing to share information when I explained I wasn't opening in competition with them.'

Calculating your prices

Establishing what you should charge on your menu means working out your food cost percentage on each dish. This does not have to be the same for everything on the menu. You calculate your food cost percentage by taking the cost of everything involved in making one dish and dividing it by your menu price.

The formula to work out menu prices is as follows:
Cost of ingredients divided by the cost percentage goal.

How it works in practice:
You have a pizza on your menu. It costs you £3.43 to make, including ingredients, staff, fuel etc. You want a food cost percentage of 40%. Take £3.43 and divide it by 0.40 to give you £8.57. For a more appealing price you should round this up or down to the nearest 25p. Giving you a final menu price of £8.50.

Let's now take a dish where the ingredients are more expensive. For example, a steak with potatoes, vegetables and a side salad. The cost of the dish to produce stands at £5.50. You want a 30% food cost percentage on it. So the calculation is £5.50 divided by 0.30, equalling £18.33, rounded to £18.50.

➡ BUDGETING

When you're working out your costs you need to plan for the first 12 months. That landmark first anniversary might seem a long way off when you're sitting there with an idea and a pile of research, but it's essential to consider not just your start-up costs but ongoing overheads for the first year. Many businesses break these down into one month, six month and then first year budgets.

Expenses

For a full budget and to see how viable your business is you'll need to balance revenue forecasts against costs. We'll come to forecasting later but it's just as crucial to work out and keep track of how much you're spending, not just the sales you hope to get through the till. Without expenses any forecasts or even sales prove very little as far as how profitable your restaurant can be. The good news is that it's far easier to work out reliable costings than revenues, especially if you veer on the side of caution.

Begin by looking at all your initial start-up costs. All the costs of getting your restaurant up and running go into the start-up expenses category. These expenses may include:

● Business registration fees
● Initial supplies
● Rent deposits
● Down payments on property
● Down payments on equipment
● Shopfitting costs
● Utility set-up fees

This is just a sample list and you probably won't have trouble adding to it once you start listing your costs.

Your operating costs are those expenses that your business will occur on an ongoing basis; essentially what you'll need to pay out each month. They may include:

- Your salary
- Staff salaries
- Rent or mortgage payments
- Telecommunications
- Utilities
- Stock
- Storage
- Distribution
- Promotion
- Loan payments
- Office supplies
- Maintenance
- Professional services (ie accountancy fees)

Again, this isn't a complete list and outgoings will vary from month to month. However, once you've completed your own lists you should have a fairly good idea, even if they're ballpark figures, of what revenues and/or funding you're going to need to support your business over a month, six month and yearly basis. These figures should go into a financial budget plan towards the end of your business plan, which also takes into account how much money you can realistically make.

Making revenue forecasts

Sales forecasting is notoriously difficult and where many business plans fall down. Almost always that's because either the business owner is hopelessly optimistic or the plan only succeeds in proving the business isn't viable because the number of sales needed to generate a profit means dishes need to be priced at an unrealistic amount for people to pay.

The biggest challenge is that you don't have any previous sales history to guide you. This is where hopefully your market research can help with examples of average turnover per square foot for similar restaurants in similar locations and of a similar size. Also consider how many people there are within certain distances and what percentage of their disposable income you can reasonably hope to secure.

However, this isn't entirely adequate as it's highly unlikely you'll perform at a similar level for perhaps up to a year. The simplest forecast is to start by working out what you hope to be making within six months. Work this out per dish served per day so you have a gross sales figure and multiply that by the number of open days in a month. Next look to scale proportionately from month one, where you're unlikely to have as many customers, upwards to month six. You can then extrapolate that scale over 12 months for an annual sales forecast.

In addition to that one forecast, carry out the process three times with a pessimistic, optimistic, and realistic outlook. Next try and put a real-time calendar next to your 'month one', 'month two' etc taking into account the peaks and troughs in trade you anticipate and is suggested from your research. Many restaurants see huge variations season-by-season, if not month-by-month.

Compiling a financial sheet

Once you've worked out your financial outgoings (both initial start-up and ongoing costs) you can put the two together to produce a clearer analysis of the viability of your restaurant on paper and when it's likely to break even. Begin by compiling month-by-month expenses and sales forecasts. In the same way you accounted for peaks and troughs in sales, look at months where you expect expenses to be higher than others. Again, ensure you prepare three income/outgoings projections: pessimistic, optimistic, realistic. Also try to account for the fact that the price you can purchase ingredients for will hopefully decrease as your sales levels increase. However, that might be a calculation you want to reserve for your optimistic forecast unless you've already got such an agreement in place from suppliers. While your calculation will inevitably alter from month-to-month (something you'll need to be wary of when managing cashflow) the point where your sales equal your expenses is where you 'break even' and hopefully go on to generate profit.

There are some formulas used to work out the break-even point:

Break-Even Point (£) = Fixed Costs ÷ Gross Margin Percentage

For example: A restaurant buys a particular bottle of wine for £10, marks it up and sells it for £20. Monthly expenses (fixed costs) are £12,000. This means our breakeven point would be £24,000 or 1,200 bottles of wine.

£12,000 ÷ (10/20) = £24,000

£24,000 ÷ £20 = 1,200

This calculation is based on that particular wine being the only product sold in the restaurant, which of course wouldn't happen, but you can substitute the cost of the wine for any number of dishes or drinks, scale up the price you sell them for until you reach your break even point.

IN MY EXPERIENCE:

Shevonne Bennett, Brown Sugar

'My plan was 82 pages long which is probably too much because the bank managers didn't want to read it all. But where it helped was by showing how I imagined Brown Sugar as a whole brand rather than just a single restaurant.'

This level of information should give you a much more powerful overview of not just how viable your business is, but what funding is required and when. It also enables you to pre-empt when you may need assistance with cashflow or credit. Having this at your fingertips won't just impress investors and the banks but should also give you a much firmer grasp on your buying decisions when it comes to actually finding and fitting out premises. But first of all, go back to the start of this section and make sure it's all safely listed in your business plan.

Things to remember:

- Don't just write your business plan for your investors, use it as your main guide for the direction of the business.

- Include all the necessary detail but don't overload it. A good plan is thorough but succinct.

- Be realistic with your sales forecasts. It's better to underestimate than overestimate.

- Have three different trading forecasts – pessimistic, optimistic and realistic.

Identity

Sculpting the identity of your business should be one of the most enjoyable challenges when starting your restaurant and is probably something you've already given a great amount of thought to. You need to do more than think about it though. It has to form a major chunk of your start-up planning.

Planning the identity of your restaurant means planning everything which will make up the experience of your customers, from the physical layout of the premises to the type of food you will serve. The other major detail you have to make a decision about is what to call your restaurant. This is where your USPs and menu may provide some assistance but the main factors to bear in mind are the impression the identity of your restaurant will make on your customers and the potential it has for branding and marketing. In the end the identity of your restaurant will be the first step in the realisation of your desire to start your own business so make sure it reflects what you set out to do in owning your own restaurant.

In this chapter we'll cover:

- Establishing your identity
- Logos and themes
- Restaurant designs
- Branding
- Business names
- Menus

WHAT IS YOUR IDENTITY?

No doubt you had a vision when you first embarked on this journey, of standing in the middle of a buzzing dining room watching your waiters serving a room full of happy customers. You shouldn't lose sight of that early vision or mental picture. It's quite possibly changed a little from the planning stage where you further identified USPs, pricing strategies and differentiators, but essentially it's still that vision, combined with these factors, that makes up your restaurant's identity.

> **IN MY EXPERIENCE:**
> ## Shevonne Bennett, Brown Sugar
>
> 'I wanted the restaurant to be a really relaxed place with a modern feel. My goal was to create a whole brand around the idea and move Caribbean food into the mainstream. It wasn't just about this one single restaurant.'

It's certainly not just the food you serve (or the prices you charge) that will determine whether you get people through the door and money through the till. You'll need to create a location and environment that pulls in customers and encourages them to spend. TGI Friday's is a popular restaurant chain often so packed you have to wait at the bar for a table even if you've booked in advance. Whether the food is worth waiting for is questionable indeed, but it's created such an exciting and inviting atmosphere, it manages to fill its tables. Too many restaurateurs don't communicate that identity, however. For some reason they have it in their head but lose sight of it when actually building the place. That's where the discipline of being a businessperson as well comes in.

Keep going back to those USPs: other than the pure food it serves, what is your restaurant? What will it look and feel like? If it's upmarket premium cuisine you're serving to a customer with a high disposable income, then the identity; from logo to location, price to platter arrangements; should reflect that. In turn, if you serve ethically sourced foods you'll want that to be entwined in all that you do. Many businesses talk about core values and entrepreneurs like to draw up a list of values that reflect their business' identity as a reminder to themselves and staff. It can certainly pay to constantly revisit them to ask: is this what we're about? Are we sticking to our USPs?

Don't neglect your USPs

Once you sacrifice your USPs – when you start diversifying your menu simply because you think you can make a nice return; compromise on quality to increase margins etc. – your restaurant stops becoming what you started it to be. This can be particularly difficult during the difficult early days of trading and fitting out, but your whole story has been built on a unique identity and losing sight of it is a major, but commonly made, mistake.

 IN MY EXPERIENCE:
Geetie Singh, The Duke of Cambridge

'I think I still have a unique proposition because it's still the only organic gastropub in the world. There are plenty of people running deeply ethical businesses and thinking their values through to the core, but not many people are doing it in the restaurant industry.'

Artistic theme and logos

You should scope out the identity of your business before you commit time or funds to a logo or an artistic theme, as they should communicate identity and your USPs to your customers at all times. Think about the famous art nouveau Pizza Express logo which has survived decades without change and still fits nicely into any high street. Sticking with the high street chains, the cartoon chicken of the Nando's logo radiates a fun and casual feel which the chain prides itself on.

Your logo is one way people will remember you and it's certainly how many customers will form their first impression. Images and colours are very powerful methods of communicating messages and you want to think carefully about the logo that should emblazon your shopfront, signage, napkins, bills, receipts, advertising, PR, company brochures and uniforms. Don't rush out and commission a brand identity group. It's often just a case of finding a logo which simply and clearly radiates your business identity.

The fuller the brief you can write about what your restaurant is, who your customers are and what you USPs are, the better a designer will be able to produce something close to what you're looking for. It's a subjective decision of course though, so it's always an idea to give an example of logos you like and don't like. A logo created by a freelance designer or small design company might give you the independent edginess that makes you stand out. For most of you you'll have no option but to pursue this route.

Another option is to ask local design colleges or students to submit entries, incentivising them with a prize or a free meal once you're open. There are a number of websites for budding, freelance or small design companies where you can pitch such competitions or request enquiries, with www.logosauce.com probably being the best. Just post your brief (remember to be as detailed as possible), set a deadline then wait for 'bidders' to upload their best efforts and contact the ones you like.

> ## ⚡ TIP
> Having a number of designs to choose from certainly helps you decide what works well, so even if you decide to give the project to one person or company ask them to give you at least a couple of options and colour schemes. You're likely to favour one and then ask to see several variations of that until you're happy.

Logos should work well in a number of sizes; whether it applies to you or not, think postage stamp and billboard. They should work well online as well as offline even if you're still in denial about the need for a website; and forward plan to ensure what works for you as a start-up will work for you as a burgeoning restaurant chain.

Making artistic themes work

One note of caution about artistic themes: don't make the mistake of thinking everyone shares your idea of good taste and smart design. They won't. This isn't your house you're choosing a theme for, it's your restaurant. While it might be 'yours' its success will be dependent on others wanting to eat there, so remember, niches are niches for a reason. Instead, apply the property development mantra: design for the broadest range of people you're looking to serve as possible.

Do your research; get out and look at how your competition style their identity and visit other restaurants to see what they get right. Also force yourself to study a successful restaurant whose identity doesn't particularly appeal to you and consider what it is that makes it work for its customers. As a rule though: create a detailed brief, get a number of designs to choose from and go with what works best for your customer, not you.

Restaurant design

We'll cover design in more detail in *Decking It Out* but it is important you have an idea of what you want for your restaurant during the planning stage. Everything from the colour of your walls to the style of furniture you pick will have an effect on the overall mood and ambience of your restaurant, and form a big chunk of its identity.

> ## ⚡ TIP
>
> Think about the kind of noise level you want in your restaurant as this will heavily influence your design. Carpets and soft furnishings absorb sound, giving a more quiet and relaxed atmosphere. However, they're harder to keep clean. Bare tables and chairs create more of a buzzy atmosphere which might be what you're after.

Give careful consideration to the little details which can also add to your identity and brand. Considerations you should bear in mind are:

- Do you want paper napkins or proper linen? More casual eateries will go for paper but you're unlikely to see anything other than proper linens in a fine dining restaurant.
- How bright should your restaurant be? Do you want softer and darker lighting for a more romantic feel or bright lights for a lively atmosphere?
- What will your food be served on? Traditional white plates, oversized bowls, wooden boards or unusually shaped dishes?
- Will your staff wear a uniform? Will this include your own branding?
- How much will you charge? We've focused on price strategy in *Planning*, but it's not just about breaking even. Your price says a lot about your identity too.

Branding

Branding differs from identity as it focuses more on what people think of your business and what it stands for. Whether you like it or not, people will form opinions on your restaurant from the minute it opens. They'll form opinions on what it looks like, the food it serves, the attitude and turnout of you and your staff. They will assign it, consciously or not, among the other brands they're exposed to.

FROM THE EXPERTS:
Simon Kossoff, Carluccio's

'We've tried as hard as possible to avoid the stereotype of a chain restaurant. There's lot's of brand elements to each restaurant but we try and keep them all a bit different.'

How much you care about branding is likely to be dependent on how much you intend to grow your business. If your sole ambition is to open one site and make a nice living from it, you probably don't need to think too much about building a brand, as simply maintaining your reputation in your local community should suffice. However, if your intentions are to one day establish a chain then branding needs to be at the forefront of your thinking. Either way, returning customers will be crucial so you should be considering how people think about your business, and that means more than just the physical site. It's the way you treat customers and how you communicate in your advertising or marketing.

Take Gordon Ramsay's restaurants as an example. They're owned and run by a foul-mouthed ex-footballer, but are still viewed as among the most prestigious restaurants in the country because of the brand he has built up, and how closely he's associated it with excellent service and unparalleled cuisine.

Deciding what your brand should stand for is about considering how you want people to view you. If you've researched your customer fully you should have a clear idea of their tastes, the kind of places they usually dine, the experiences they like and in turn don't like, and that should give you a clear steer on how you look to position your brand to them and the outside world.

Branding for you as a start-up restaurateur shouldn't be a massive pre-occupation but as it's closely aligned to identity, and your overall sales story, it's a very worthwhile exercise trying to draw up a list of words you'd like others to describe you with. This will make a useful reference document to refer back to when making buying decisions and help form marketing decisions and, eventually, a fuller branding strategy.

➡ CHOOSING A NAME

Considering it's one of the least technical aspects of starting a business, picking a name for your restaurant could prove frustratingly tricky. For some of you, owning a place with your name above the door was part of the dream from day one or the name could have been core to the vision; but for others you'll agonise over it, then kick yourself relentlessly for wasting time over something that will eventually seem so obvious.

Business names are funny things and their importance polarises opinion. It's easy to understand the ambiguity. Think of any favourite restaurant you eat in, and in almost every instance, the name is the very last consideration and least important factor in your conscious decision for liking it.

IN MY EXPERIENCE:
Shevonne Bennett, Brown Sugar

'I had an original name in my head but it just didn't feel right. Then one day I was watching a film called Brown Sugar and it suddenly just clicked.'

That said, business names are how we all identify and refer to those establishments and it's often what we remember most. And while some names bear little significance to anything, the smartest names undoubtedly form part of the branding and identity that pulls us in. Let's take Yo! Sushi as an example. The name suggests the experience you'll get when you eat in the restaurant will be modern and definitely a bit more lively than your average Japanese-style eatery. A strong choice of name has also allowed founder Simon Woodroffe to apply 'Yo!' to other brands, most recently to Yotel, a chain of pod-like hotel rooms found at Gatwick and Heathrow.

So how important are business names? Well, it's safe to assume that you won't improve a bad restaurant with a great name, and a place shouldn't suffer too badly from an average moniker. Essentially, what you cook, for what price and how good your service is, will determine whether people like your venue or not.

But that doesn't mean names aren't important. A good name will:

- Draw attention and attract people through the door
- Communicate a clear message about your restaurant's identity
- Lend itself well to PR and set you aside from the competition

A poor one will hinder all of the above. So they're the basic principles you should work on when planning a name.

Regional names can work if you don't have aspirations of expanding or relocating. Locals might consider they're supporting a town's trade if you carry its name. If you're serving dishes in an area renowned for its produce it also makes sense to take advantage of that reputation.

✦ TIP

If you decide to incorporate your business you need to make sure you pick a name nobody else has. If you run your business as a sole trader this is not as much of an issue but you still need to be aware of the legal implications of choosing an offensive moniker, or one with certain banned words. Check *Registering Your Business* for more on the legal aspects of choosing a name.

Making it web friendly

You'll also need to think about web presence when considering the suitability of a name. It's so easy and cheap to get a website to publicise your business that you'd be foolish not to consider it as a future option. When thinking about names that'll work on the internet, think search. Nine-tenths of visitors to all websites arrive at them via a search engine (i e Google). Some names will work well for restaurants, but will impact differently in search. Regional names will allow locals to find your website when they search with location included. However, it can also work against you. If you're called Clapham Tandoori, you're sure to appear for a 'Clapham + Tandoori' search but will you get lost among all the other results? Here a unique name could work to ensure you appear, get seen and people can also find you when they type in your name.

To the other extreme, don't make the mistake of naming your company simply because it's a well-searched word or term. It's not about appearing on the most searches, just the right ones and near enough to the top. Avoid obvious clangers too. A press release once arrived in the Startups.uk office from a new business selling a product which safely adjusted adult seatbelts for children. It sounded like a decent enough product with market potential but further down the press release the name was finally revealed to be 'Cruising4Kids', which undoubtedly wasn't the kind of message the entrepreneur wanted to put across to his customers!

With all this in mind, possibly the best bet is how most entrepreneurs say they came up with their business' name: brainstorming around a table, preferably in a pub or, if at home, with a glass of wine. Set those creative juices flowing and see what you can come up with. The obvious place to start is semantics. Find a word that encompasses what your restaurant represents.

Whatever you do, don't waste your money paying someone to come up with a name: there's no shortage of companies that will do this but it's simply not a wise way to spend money as a start-up. If you're still not convinced, take heed from Royal Mail's calamitous multi-million pound rebrand to Consignia. It's a fair bet if Royal Mail had taken a tenth of the money it paid for the rebrand and offered it to its staff to come up with a new identity, they'd have though of something a lot better.

 # MENU

Your restaurant can have the most romantic, candlelit atmosphere of every restaurant on the high street, or be the coolest hang-out with the funkiest design and hippest music in the background. If you haven't got a decent menu though, all other novelties will wear thin very quickly with your customers. Your restaurant *is* your menu.

IN MY EXPERIENCE:
Shevonne Bennett, Brown Sugar

'When it came to putting together my menu I got various ideas from friends, family and other people I knew. They gave me lists of dishes they liked and I chose the ones I liked best and added new ones myself.'

Type of food

For most restaurateurs, the type of food they intend to serve when dreaming up ideas for a new restaurant forms the basis of their whole concept. The whole business revolves around the type and origin of the cuisine on offer. For others, the idea stems more from the concept of the restaurant – a new approach to service, an entertaining accompaniment to meals, an unforgettable style of décor. If your big idea revolves more around the physical restaurant than the food itself, you need to give special consideration to your menu choices from a very early stage as they won't come as naturally to you.

The majority of restaurants position themselves in the market by serving one type of cuisine – Chinese, Italian, Mexican etc – but increasing numbers of restaurateurs are building their menus around the combined influences of several different countries or even continents. There's nothing wrong with this, and indeed it can work extremely well, as long you keep it simple and hire a chef capable of embracing all those different styles and preparing a variety of dishes to a consistent standard.

Taking the specialised route can do wonders for your customer base however. Focusing on special diets such as vegetarian, vegan or religious requirements can give you a unique selling proposition. There has been a rise in recent years of Halal and Kosher restaurants serving other kinds of ethnic foods, such as Chinese. If you go down this route however, you'll need to consider your location carefully and make sure there's enough of a customer base in the area.

IN MY EXPERIENCE:
Ian Pengelley, Gilgamesh

'You need to be aware of where you're getting your ingredients from when you're putting your menu together, such as using sustainable fish in your dishes. Customers care about that now so you need to.'

The shortlist

Deciding on the dishes you want to end up on the menu is no easy process. Start by making a list of everything you're considering, no matter how long it is. Then you can start to asses what on the list fits in with the concept of your restaurant. Once you've got a list of dishes that suit your theme, you need to start trying them out, either yourself or through your chef, if you already have one at this stage. Some dishes may read well on a menu and taste fantastic, but if they're too complex to make, and can't be prepared to order, it can cause chaos in the kitchen during a busy service.

The size of your menu is also crucial. The more high-end you want your restaurant to be, the smaller your menu will be. You'll be hard pressed to find a kitchen with 25 different main dishes on it that are all cooked fresh, and to a high standard every night. Ask yourself if you need more than six or seven choices. That number of dishes gives you plenty of scope for variety. Within that number you can have four meat dishes, and still have room for a couple of fish and vegetarian options.

TIP

A small menu can be perfected. A large menu lacks quality control. And remember, you can always have a couple of specials written up on a board that change daily or weekly.

If you've got a chef on board at this stage you should be consulting them on menu decisions as they're the one that has to cook up your grand ideas. If you don't have enough culinary experience you may have to leave most menu planning to your chefs anyway, but you have to make sure you take an active role in the decision-making and sample all the dishes yourself before anything gets printed. We'll talk more about updating your menus in *Surviving the First six Months*.

IN MY EXPERIENCE:

Geetie Singh, The Duke of Cambridge

'I'd been a restaurateur for a long time so right from the beginning I knew what I wanted from my own restaurant. It was going to serve bloody good ingredients-driven food, have a short simple menu, and be extremely fresh. The menu would change every day, using local seasonal ingredients.'

Menu design

What your menu looks like from a style point of view will be dictated by your brand and general restaurant design. Restaurants like TGI Friday's have lots of photographs and images within their menus but as a rule, avoid photos like the plague – it cheapens your whole proposition. Images are for catalogues. The descriptions of each dish should be enough to entice the diners. Make your mantra 'keep it simple'.

Avoid plastic or laminated menus unless you're going for a fast food feel to the place. A crisp off-white coloured card can look great and also informs your customers that the menu is regularly updated.

TIP

Try to include any particularly strong-flavoured ingredients in the dish descriptions. While some people love flavours such as fennel or coriander, others find them really off-putting in their food so it's best to let them know so they can make appropriate menu choices.

Other menu design considerations include:

- Being descriptive on your menu, but not too much. You don't want to be filling pages and pages with long and unnecessary details about how things have been prepared
- Having a clear distinction between starters and mains so your customers know exactly what they're ordering
- Advertising the origins of your ingredients if they're from local sources or a particularly well-known farm or location

Things to remember:

- Remember that identity must go hand-in-hand with every aspect of your planning, from décor to menu price.

- Keep your branding as consistent as possible.

- Don't agonise over your restaurant's name but do give it careful consideration.

- Keep your menu as simple, short and clear as possible.

Finance 1: Start-up funding

The internet has allowed a whole generation of entrepreneurs to make their millions with virtually no start-up capital. Unfortunately, the restaurant industry is not one where you can start trading without significant financial investment in the venture, and the support of a great bank manager, so you're going to need to consider your funding opportunities carefully.

Although the prospect of making a presentation to a bank to convince them to fund your venture can seem daunting, this chapter outlines everything you need to do to prepare, from reviewing your business plan to what you should wear and how to cope if you hear that dreaded 'no'. Also covered are other means of finance which you should consider such as loans from friends and family or private equity finance, and how to protect yourself and your business if you choose this option.

In this chapter we'll cover:

- Funding options
- Banks
- Friends and family loans
- Equity finance
- Applying for a loan
- Pitching for finance
- Paying yourself

➡ FINANCE OPTIONS

Restaurants need money, and in relatively large quantities too. If you're looking to start a business with few barriers to entry, only have a couple of thousand to spend and don't want to borrow anything, then you should probably start considering other industries. There's no getting away from the fact it's going to cost you a pretty penny to get up and running and will also involve substantial overheads. However, there's no reason, if you've done thorough research and planning, you shouldn't successfully access the finance you need to start up.

It's likely you'll have three funding options for opening a restaurant. The first is to fund it yourself, the second to use a bank, the third to seek equity investment from private investors. It's highly unlikely you'll raise venture capital finance to start your first restaurant; possibly to roll-out a chain but not to start the first.

IN MY EXPERIENCE:

Geetie Singh, The Duke of Cambridge

'We did a lot of networking trying to raise the cash. We used Business Link and found a business angel organisation that linked us with a lot of people that may have wanted to invest in us.'

Funding it yourself

Funding it yourself should be a fairly simple decision: either you can or you can't. There really is no such thing as free money so for pure efficiency nothing makes better financial sense than resisting borrowing altogether. Of course it's an option few are blessed with. It's also an option some are distinctly uncomfortable with. Do you really want to invest your life savings into a venture when it's possible to borrow from a bank? Possibly not. If that's the case, the first question to ask is if you're not convinced, why should any other form of investor be? The second is, how much can you comfortably put in? Banks are likely to expect you to match whatever they lend you and you'll do well to find an individual who'll give you their cash to play with while you keep your own in the bank.

> ### ✦ TIP
> It can actually be sensible to fund start-up costs with a loan and save a slice of your own cash for running costs and future investment; borrowing for a loan will be less expensive than an overdraft or credit cards. There could also be tax advantages to structuring how much you invest yourself but you'll probably need an accountant to help with structuring this.

Friends and family

'Fools' is often jokingly tagged onto the end of this duo and not just for its alliterative appeal. Start-up businesses are risky investments when they're backed by even the canniest of high-yielding, wealthy business veterans. Yet strangely, people seem willing to part with princely sums for decisions based on little more than emotion, love and the conviction someone they believe in will look after their money.

As you're the one looking for the money, not blindly pumping it in, this might not concern you. Indeed, it's easy to turn the situation on its head and convince them that you're actually doing them a favour by letting them share in your inevitable success. If all goes well, this could be true. It's what happens if it doesn't that you need to consider. Many friendships and relationships have gone out of the window as the bailiffs have walked in through the door, so think carefully about selling too hard to friends and family. Explain the risks, get any investment tied up in a legally binding contract securing both your rights and express no matter how much you try to make this work you can't guarantee them it will. If after doing all this, both sides are happy then by all means go ahead. Funding from friends and family, when it works, is certainly a massive leg up and leaves you the freedom to save bank financing for a later stage when you're looking to expand and grow.

IN MY EXPERIENCE:
Geetie Singh, The Duke of Cambridge

'We needed £250,000 in total, but I had a friend who was willing to invest from the beginning. We had the first £60,000 from him. It made it a lot easier to pitch for the rest.'

Equity finance

Before we look at banks, which are how most of you will probably fund the opening of your restaurant, it is worth touching on equity finance. Private equity usually comes from one or more private wealthy individuals, commonly known as business angels, who are often experienced entrepreneurs with money to invest in other up-and-coming companies. While the reality is far removed from the drama of the TV show, these are the kind of deals struck on the BBC hit series *Dragons' Den*.

TIP

Equity finance is where you give away a percentage of your business in exchange for the money you require to start or grow.

It's also possible to raise equity finance through organised public or private funds, which are usually run by either experienced entrepreneurs or investment companies. Private equity deals usually fill the gap between standard bank loans and venture capital deals, but can vary from anything from £10,000 to £250,000. Venture capital works on the same principal but is run by large organisations and deals are usually in excess of £500,000, rarely for start-up businesses, even rarer for new restaurants and the venture capital funding organisation will usually place someone on the company's board.

Private equity is certainly more common but not easy to find, and not always the advised route for initial start-up capital. A more recognised route is to start one restaurant using debt finance, perfect the business model and develop evidence of the business' potential to expand and then refinance using private equity. At that point, with solid evidence of sales, market and product supply, far more investors are likely to be interested. However, if you've run a restaurant or business before, or have a proven track record in the sector it might be that you'll find an investor willing to take a punt on you from day one.

> ### ✦ TIP
> There's one thing all advisers agree on. If you can keep 100% to start with, then do so. Those in the investment world will no doubt argue it's way smarter to own 50% of a company worth £1m than 100% of one worth £100,000 – and clearly that's true. The problem is that whatever you're giving away at the start won't be worth very much, so it's almost certain you'll lose a chunky slice at what in a few years time might seem a meagre sum. It's far better to use debt finance and then refinance once you're in a better position to bargain from and can offer a greater chance of reward for the investor's risk.

Taking on an equity partner also provides a new sense of responsibility and pressure. With the money comes a need to create a substantial return in an agreed period of time, and once you commit to that the decisions you make must become more focussed on generating that return than what works for you in a lifestyle scenario. That can be a very healthy motivation but it's only worth it if that's the type of business you want to run.

Bank or debt finance

Banks lent £33.3bn to small businesses in 2006 and contrary to the doom and gloom surrounding the state of the economy are still very much lending to people like you starting independent restaurants. As such they should be the first place you look when looking to finance your shop. Banks are vastly experienced in helping start-up businesses and should be able to offer a number of finance packages tailored to your needs as well as a fair degree of support. A good bank manager should be able to give you a clear explanation of your options and what is expected to meet any lending criteria.

> ### ✦ TIP
> Be warned, banks know restaurant models inside out so will see through any overly optimistic forecasts, dressing up of figures or holes in your business plan so you'll need to ensure your research is comprehensive.

➡ GETTING THE MONEY

Choosing a bank

It's natural that you'll probably turn to your current bank first – and you shouldn't apologise for that. If you have a good relationship with your bank manager it's natural to want to choose their branch to open a business account with. However, even if you're keen to stay with your main bank, do shop around and examine the start-up packages on offer if only to check you're not missing out on something available elsewhere. If you spot a deal, you can always negotiate with your existing bank manager to match it.

Different banks offer different incentives such as so many years' free banking to open a business bank account, as well as pricing and organising their charging mechanisms differently. Some offer a greater level of service and usually offer lower interest rates or higher charges as a result, while other banks specialise in keeping basic costs low but offering little service. While there are savings it's likely you'll ultimately derive more long-term value from finding a bank you're comfortable with; who makes the effort to listen, understands your business and ultimately, will lend you the money you need to start-up.

 FROM THE EXPERTS:
Iqbal Wahhab, The Cinnamon Club and Roast

'Only a tiny amount of the £2.5m needed for the Cinnamon Club came from myself. I got £1m from the bank. Luckily I found a bank manager called Paul Cinnamon. I wrote to him and said: "we need to talk and you'll soon understand why". Convincing investors was a lot more difficult. I'd pitch this great idea for a restaurant to people who'd say "that's great, but what kind of experience do you have in the industry?" So I did get a few knock-backs in the early days.'

Contending with bank managers

Even if you're decided on a bank offering make sure you meet the bank manager you'll be dealing with. The relationship with your bank manager is absolutely fundamental to your success, especially in raising finance. Managers will have a threshold of loans they can sign off and even though you'll be assessed by the bank's credit and decisions programmes, having your manager on side will make a massive difference. Bear in mind that bank managers will vary within banks not just from bank to bank. If you like a package at one bank but don't click with the manager, ask to see another. Alternatively, check your manager is experienced in your sector and within your focus area; it could make a difference.

IN MY EXPERIENCE:

Shevonne Bennett, Brown Sugar

'I was denied again and again by the banks. They just couldn't see past my lack of experience, despite the fact that they loved my business plan. I ended up going through investors and using my parents as guarantors on a personal loan.'

Applying for a bank loan

Bank loans remain the most common and preferred type of finance for opening restaurants. The nature of acquiring and fitting out premises and equipment, on top of all the operational costs associated with starting any business, make restaurants cash-intensive to start up and quite often too much of an undertaking for someone to make on their own. The upside is that the banks are familiar with financing loans for restaurants. They know the business models inside out and you won't have to try and convince them of a whole new concept or sector. The downside to this is that banks also have very clear expectations of what they expect to see from your business plan before they'll give you a penny and it's crucial you bear this in mind.

They'll want to see you've factored for all eventualities, your own income and been realistic about your anticipated revenues. Some entrepreneurs will tell you it's sometimes best to have two sets of figures: a real one for yourself and a dressed up one for the bank. That might work for industries such as the internet and web 2.0 where business models are still new and revenues emerging all the time, but banks know restaurants so any gilding of the lily is unlikely to wash.

> ## TIP
>
> The banks will have a clear criteria you'll be expected to meet for them to be convinced they'll see a return on their investment and if you're at all unsure about your forecasts or figures it's worth speaking to a bank manager before submitting any loan application to see if you're along the right line or need to have a rethink.

Depending on how much you want to borrow, banks will usually expect to see that you're matching what you're borrowing with your own money and could also ask for security against your home. This is something that puts many people off and can seem understandably frightening. If you reach this point and are having second thoughts, you're possibly not ready to start a business after all. What you're about to do is indeed high risk. However, providing it works it's also full of rewards. If you're not convinced that balance is in your favour you have to ask why the bank should lend you money.

> ## TIP
>
> If you can't offer the security the bank is asking for, you could apply for a loan through the government's Small Firms Loans Guarantee Scheme which guarantees bank loans up to £250,000 and while notoriously bureaucratic and inconsistent in its outcome, is welcomed by all the main banks and did support more than £200m worth of loans last year.

If you're reluctant or unable to offer security or match the banks lending, the other option is to lower the amount you want to borrow. Providing you have a decent credit rating and can offer reasonable evidence you'll be able to afford the repayments, banks will often give personal loans up to around £15,000 which can be used for start-up costs and repaid over 36–84 months.

Banks will also offer you credit card and overdraft facilities, but will discourage you from using them for anything other than cashflow management and short-term borrowing. That's not to say you can't use them however you see fit but, especially in the current climate, be very careful about borrowing anything you couldn't afford to pay back at very short notice or you could find yourself in real trouble over a relatively small amount.

IN MY EXPERIENCE:

Geetie Singh, The Duke of Cambridge

'NatWest said they'd give us £100,000 and we got the rest from a couple of private investors. But three weeks before we were due to open we got a call late at night from NatWest telling us the woman who'd given us the loan hadn't got authorisation and it'd been turned down. That was AA our first lessons: Get everything in writing and don't trust what you've been told. We then had a week to raise the extra money. We just knocked on everybody's door and eventually got it through more private investors.'

Pitching for finance

Before we get into the detail of what you should say, how you should dress and what banks and investors expect when you pitch for finance, it's important to highlight one all-important, and too often overlooked fact about borrowing money: banks (and investors) want to lend it. Regardless of how bad the economic climate gets, banks and investors will always lend money if they're confident they'll get a healthy return. Your challenge then isn't to beg and grovel for any scrap of money you can get your hands on, but to present a compelling opportunity for them.

It's on this premise you should base your pitch. Remember banks are investing other people's money so they need to, as far as is possible, guarantee a return. They're certainly not gamblers. Your challenge then is to present a clear, low-risk proposition that demonstrates how the money will be spent and, crucially, how it'll be repaid and when.

Preparation

Make sure you're 100% prepared. If you're actually making a presentation, be clear about all your facts and figures and know them off by heart. It's likely that a bank will have already read your business plan by the time you get to pitch or talk through your proposition. View this stage as good news that the bank wants to talk further. However, think what else they might want to ask you. Critique your own business plan or ask others to do it for you with a view to pre-empting any questions that stand out.

A clear concise answer will reassure the bank that you're clear about what you're doing and that this matters to you sufficiently to have put the effort in. Don't attempt to try and answer a question if you can't; this only sends a message that you'll try and fudge. All investors prefer honesty so be honest and admit you don't know, but suggest you could certainly find out. Perhaps even flatter them by thanking them for bringing it your attention.

Appearance

It's important to dress smartly too. It's unfortunate, but the fact is how you dress not how talented you are or how great your business idea is might determine if you get a bank loan. Wearing a suit demonstrates a professionalism and desire to be taken seriously. Whatever your personal view, the majority of bank managers will still expect you to dress smartly so neglecting to do so is risky. If you're someone who simply couldn't bear to change their appearance then by all means dress as you see fit, but be aware one of the most important attributes of a small business owner needs to be flexibility and your reluctance to adapt could be viewed as representative of your personality.

Dealing with a No

Rejection is something you should get used to quickly though. There's every chance several banks will say no before one says yes. See each rejection as a learning experience or rehearsal for the one that says yes. Find out why they've said no, the feedback might be useful. Don't let it dampen your spirits though, there's always more money out there. And don't argue with the decision either. Disputing a bank's decision to say no is as futile as arguing with refereeing decisions; you're never going to change their minds.

FROM THE EXPERTS:
Simon Kossoff, Carluccio's

'We had to raise a couple of million to get the business going but it was a very difficult time. It took us nearly two years. It was around the dotcom era and I think it would have been easier for us to raise £200m for an online food business than a bricks and mortar venture. We must have done about 100 presentations but the VCs just weren't interested. But eventually we started getting some interest from angels and slowly started to secure the cash we needed.'

Paying yourself

Your business plan should include how and what you intend to pay yourself for at least the first year – and it's essential you include this in any borrowing that you take out. It's true that banks and investors love to see you're making massive sacrifices to see your business get off the ground. If you can afford not to take a salary for the first few months, even year, they'll expect you to do this. It not only ensures all profits can be reinvested back into the business, but demonstrates just how badly you want to succeed. However, it's simply impossible for many people to do unless you're wealthy enough to have six months' salary in the bag. If you can't survive without taking a salary out of the business, whatever you do, don't pretend you can. Trying not to pay yourself and hoping you'll somehow muddle through almost never works and is foolish to try.

Everybody has to pay a mortgage or rent; everybody has to eat; everybody has reasonable living expenses – and lenders do understand that. Not paying yourself a wage will just mean you end up borrowing elsewhere and, conversely, lenders can actually view that as bad management. Saying you can live on £500 a month when your mortgage is £1,000 isn't going to look too clever. Lenders also dislike it when they lend an initial amount of money based on forecasts they've been told are realistic only for the borrower to promptly return needing more. Again that doesn't speak much for management.

It's far better to include your wage as a cost of the business. Indeed, it actually sets your business out on a solid model from the outset. Anyone who stepped into your shoes or acquired the business would expect to either earn a wage or pay a managing director a wage and your business model needs to be able to support that. For example, a business that claims to be generating a healthy profit of £50,000 but whose owners are effectively working for free, perhaps isn't as successful as it might first appear. That said, don't expect to pay yourself a fortune. If you're coming from a corporate background to escape the pressured rate race, be realistic. You're moving into hospitality and should expect to earn a hospitality salary.

> ### ⭐ TIP
> There are very few statistics for average earnings, but look at the average earnings of advertised posts for restaurant managers and try and come in somewhere just below.

Things to remember:

- Consider your finance options carefully. What's best for you, straight loans or giving away a share of the pie?

- Make sure family and friends are clear about what they're getting involved in before you accept any cash from them.

- Be prepared when pitching. You need to know your figures inside out.

- Be realistic. It's better to ask for the cash in advance than ask for help when you're in trouble.

Things to consider when financing a new restaurant

1. How much finance is required?

First, you need to identify the equipment you require and the equipment suppliers you wish to use. It's possible to finance all catering equipment, furniture and fittings for your restaurant. The general rule is: 'If it's for business use, it can be financed'. Make sure you factor everything you need including building works/kitchen fabrication into your plan. Once you have a rough idea of total set up cost, you can look to secure finance. It's possible to approve finance within 24 hours. For a new start restaurant, it's possible to approve anything from £1,000 to £250,000.

2. What information is required?

In order to secure finance, you'll need to supply basic information about yourself and your business. This information includes: what you want to finance, the amount of finance you require, your home address, date of birth, proposed opening date etc. If you have any other information that will support your application, now is the time to provide it. Examples of supporting information include: business plan, financial projections and details of your personal investment in the restaurant. At this stage you'll also need to confirm whether you're looking for finance over 3, 4 or 5 years.

3. What happens next?

Once you've provided all the relevant information about the business, you'll need to wait for formal finance approval (typically 24 hours). Once approved, paperwork is posted out directly for you sign. Once you've signed and returned paperwork, payment can be made directly to your chosen suppliers via bank transfer. The whole process from initial phone call to release of cleared funds can be completed within 7 days. Your monthly payments are fixed (inflation resistant) and 100% tax deductible. Payments are processed monthly by direct debit from a nominated account.

To talk to Portman Asset Finance about your new business, call on **0844 800 88 25**. Alternatively visit **www.portmanassetfinance.co.uk**

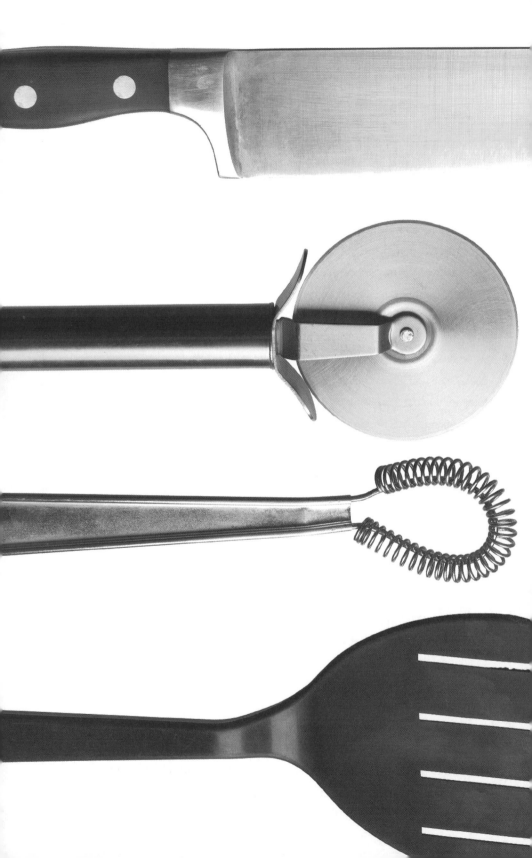

Setting up

Registering your business

S omething you'll need to give some thought to before you even look for a premises or start designing your menus is the business structure for your restaurant. There are several choices available to you. Some involve more paperwork; others are more suited to businesses of a certain size. We outline the different legal structures your business can follow, be that as a sole trader, with a partner, or as a limited company. Also covered are the costs involved, the paperwork you need to submit and any appointments you'll need to make.

Although it may not be one of your strengths, anyone with the determination to actually set up their own business has a chance to succeed. Your passion may be food but you've simply got to get to grips with business structure if you want to run a restaurant.

In this chapter we'll cover:

- Sole traders and partnerships
- Limited companies
- Registering as a limited company

THE DIFFERENT LEGAL STRUCTURES

There are essentially three legal or accounting structures you can choose from when starting your restaurant. You can go it alone by being a sole trader, team up to form a partnership or operate a limited company. Choosing the right structure is important, so you'll need to give it some thought. However, it is possible to switch between different structures after you've started your restaurant. For example, you may start out as a sole trader, and then decide to register your business as a limited company or partnership. You will save yourself a lot of work if you establish the most appropriate business structure beforehand though. Below is an explanation of the different legal structures you can choose from when starting your restaurant and guidance on which structure is most suitable for your restaurant.

Sole traders and partnerships

Registering as a sole trader is relatively straightforward, record keeping is simple and you get to keep all the profits after tax. As a sole trader you are the single owner of the business and have complete control over the way it is run. However, the law makes no distinction between the business and you as the owner, which means any debt can be met from your own personal wealth if the business runs into trouble. If you choose to run your restaurant as a sole trader you must also register as self-employed with HMRC within three months of your trading start date, otherwise you could be fined and charged interest on any outstanding tax and National Insurance payments you owe.

When two or more people combine to form a business unit this is called a partnership. As with the sole trader model, each partner is responsible for any debts the business incurs. Each partner is also self-employed and receives a percentage of any returns from the business, which they are then taxed on. The partnership, as well as the individuals within it, must submit annual self-assessment returns to HMRC and keep stringent records on business income and expenses.

Starting a restaurant as a sole trader or partnership venture may prove the easier option in the short-term. There is less paperwork involved and you will not need to register and send annual returns to Companies House. It is also much easier to withdraw funds from the business as essentially, all profits make up your own earnings. However, as well as the financial liability that lies at your feet as a sole trader, it is much more difficult to grow the business and you may find it harder when dealing with creditors and suppliers.

Limited liability companies

Registering as a limited (Ltd) company is probably the best legal structure to go with if you have any intention of growing your business. As well as offering you a degree of personal financial security should your restaurant run into financial difficulty, it will also give your business more credibility when seeking finance or credit. Registering your restaurant business as a limited company also makes tax and succession planning a lot easier.

If you expect your restaurant to maintain a healthy amount of trade and return high levels of profit you will definitely want to go with the Ltd model. Profits will be subject to corporation tax, which currently stands at half the 40% income tax rate you could end up paying as a high-earning sole trader. Limited companies pay corporation tax on profits and company directors are taxed as employees in the same way that any other people you employ, such as chefs and waiting staff, are taxed.

A limited company is very different from a sole trader model where there is no legal distinction between you and the business. A limited company is a separate legal entity to the people that run it. Profits and losses belong to the company, and the business can continue regardless of the death, resignation or bankruptcy of the shareholders or directors. Your personal financial risk will be restricted to how much you have invested in the company and any guarantees you gave when raising finance for the business. However, if the company fails and you have not carried out your duties as a company director, you could be liable for debts as well as being disqualified from acting as a director in another company.

If you decide to register your restaurant as a limited company you will need to allow more time to deal with the paperwork as it is a much more administration heavy process than running a business as a sole trader. It will also require most stringent record keeping and auditing throughout the entire life of the business.

➡ REGISTERING AS A LIMITED COMPANY

To register your restaurant as a limited company you must submit the appropriate paperwork to Companies House, the official UK government register of UK companies. You can download more detailed instructions and the appropriate application forms at www.companieshouse.gov.uk. What follows is a guide to the process, documents and requirements involved in turning your business into a legal entity.

Although it is possible to register a limited company yourself, unless you have done it before you are probably going to need to engage the services of either a solicitor, accountant, chartered secretary or a company formation agent. Formation agents use their own software that works directly with the Companies House systems. If you want to register your company electronically (most are registered this way) you will need to have the specific Companies House electronic interface – hence the need for a formation agent. However, you can still deliver the physical documents directly to Companies House without the need of a formation agent or specific electronic interface.

IN MY EXPERIENCE:

Shevonne Bennett, Brown Sugar

'We traded as a limited company and it was quite straightforward to register. I did it myself with the help of a formation agent. The whole process was pretty simple and probably cost me about £100 in total.'

Costs

Prices for formation agents can cost anything up to £200, depending on the level of service you require. A key advantage of using a formation agent is the advice they can give you on the compiling of the necessary documents and the right structure for your business. Companies House does not provide this service when registering, so if you are unfamiliar with the process it is advisable to get help to avoid errors. Going through the registration process yourself can be time-consuming, especially if you make a mistake, and Companies House staff will not advise you about specific matters such as the content of the documents you are required to submit.

Alternatively, you could also get assistance from an online registration company. The standard service usually costs £80–£100 including fees, but since some documentation needs to be posted, registration takes three to eight days. This option is usually cheaper than using a formation agent, although you will not receive the same level of personal service.

Finally, you can buy an 'off the shelf' company. You will receive a ready-made limited company that has designated company officers listed on the paperwork. You simply transfer your name, and the names of any other company directors once you receive your documentation. The process can be completed on the same day and many accountancy firms will have several ready-made limited companies which they can sell to you. This is the quickest option, and, with the exception of registering the company yourself, can often be the cheapest too.

Company officers

Once you have agreed whether or not you need help in establishing your company you will need to decide on who the company officers will be, and what your business will be called.

Limited companies are required by law to have named company officers. Company officers are the formally named directors and company secretary as stated in the Articles of Association, one of the documents you submit to Companies House which is explained in more detail below. It is a legal requirement for company officers to be in place at all times and for their names and current addresses to be written on the registration documents. If there is a change in company officers, Companies House must be informed straight away. All private limited companies must have at least one director and a company secretary.

Company directors – these are the people that manage the company's affairs in accordance with its Articles of Association and the law. Generally, anyone can be appointed company director and the post does not require any formal qualifications. However, there are a few exceptions.

You are prohibited from being a company director if:

- You are an undischarged bankrupt or disqualified by a court from holding a directorship
- You are under 16 (this only applies in Scotland)

Company directors have a responsibility to make sure certain documents reach the registrar at Companies House. These are:

- Accounts
- Annual returns
- Notice of change of directors or secretaries
- Notice of change of registered office

Directors that fail to deliver these documents on time can be prosecuted and are subject to fines of up to £5,000 for each offence. On average, 1,000 directors are prosecuted each year for failing to deliver accounts and returns on time so it is not a responsibility that can be taken lightly or ignored.

Company secretary – this person's duty is not specified by law but usually contained within an employment contract. For private limited companies, secretaries are not required to have any special qualifications.

The main duties of a company secretary are to:

- Maintain the statutory registers
- Ensure statutory forms are filed promptly
- Provide members and auditors with notice of meetings
- Send the Registrar copies of resolutions and agreements
- Supply a copy of the accounts to every member of the company
- Keep or arrange minutes of meetings

Naming your business

As well as establishing your company officers, you will also need to pick a company name to register the business with. The name of your business does not have to be the same as the name of your restaurant however. If you open three restaurants, all with different names, you can still run them as one limited company. You will need to establish your company name before you think about filling out your registration documents as there are certain rules to consider.

The name you choose for your company must:

- Feature the word 'limited' or 'ltd' at the end. For Welsh companies the equivalent 'cyfyngedig' or 'cyf' can be used, but documentation must also state in English that it is a limited company
- Not be made up of certain sensitive words or expressions (listed by Companies House) without the consent of the Secretary of State or relevant government department

- Not imply a connection with central or local government
- Not be offensive
- Not be the same or similar to one that appears in the Index of Names kept by Companies House

You can search the index of business names already registered on the Companies House website free of charge. If your chosen name is too similar to another, an objection can be lodged within 12 months following the incorporation of your company and you could forced to change it. For more on the creative side of choosing your name, see the chapter on *Identity*.

Documents to submit

When registering a limited company there are four documents which must be provided to Companies House. These are:

Memorandum of Association

This document sets out the following:

- The company's name
- Where the company's registered office is located – England, Wales or Scotland
- What the company will do – this can be as simple as: 'to conduct business as a general commercial company'

Articles of Association

Here is where you set out the rules for running your company. You must state how shares will be allocated and transferred, how the directors, the secretary and your meetings will be governed. And if you decide not to adopt the standard articles of the Companies Act in full (known as Table A) you have to submit your amended version when registering. Once your company is incorporated you can only make changes if the holders of 75% of the voting rights in your company agree, so it pays to get this right at the outset.

Form 10

This document gives details of the first director(s), company secretary and the address of the registered office. Company directors must also give their name, address, date of birth, occupation and details of other directorships held in the last five years.

Form 12

This document is the statutory declaration of compliance with all the legal requirements of the incorporation of a company. It must be signed by either one of the company directors or secretary named on Form 10, or the solicitor forming the company. The signing of the document must be witnessed by a solicitor, a commissioner for oaths, a justice of the peace or a notary public. Form 12 must not be signed and dated before any of the other documents are completed, signed and dated.

Once all that's been submitted your restaurant is a fully fledged limited company, but don't forget: the legal structure you choose when you start trading isn't set in stone. You can alter your structure, or even float on the stock market should your business become successful enough.

Things to remember:

- Assess your business structure options carefully. It may be cheaper to stay as a sole trader but are the risks to your personal finances worth it?

- When registering as a limited company make sure you've gone over your documents meticulously before submitting them. If you make a mistake you'll have to submit them again.

- Search the list of submitted business names on the Companies House website before you get your heart set on one. It may not be available.

2.2
Finding property

The premises you choose will have a massive impact not just on the look, feel and atmosphere of your restaurant, but also on the success of your business. It's probably the most important single decision you have to make in the whole start-up process, so make sure you give it careful consideration.

You must decide what you need from your premises – in terms of size and layout and also in terms of how the location of your restaurant will impact on your profits. Once you have decided what type of property and what kind of area suit your needs you'll need to decide whether leasing or buying is best for you. There are advantages to both but for many, finance will be the key factor. This chapter also covers the legal issues of securing your premises such as the commercial classification and what kind of professional advice you should seek before moving forward on any decision.

In this chapter we'll cover:

- What you need from a property
- Location
- Commercial classifications
- Leasing vs buying
- Professional advisors

WHAT ARE YOUR PROPERTY NEEDS?

At this stage you should already have a clear idea of what you require from your restaurant premises. You will already have decided on the type of clientele you want to attract and the kind of atmosphere you want to create. All these decisions will have a bearing on where you locate your restaurant, what size it needs to be and how much you're willing to pay for your bricks and mortar.

Property will be your single biggest expense. Another reason to think carefully about the building you start your restaurant in is it's not easy to change your mind once you've made a decision.

Staff are easy enough to replace. Suppliers can be changed. However, if you're not happy with your premises, or you find it isn't suitable once you open, you'll have a tough job on your hands trying to relocate.

 IN MY EXPERIENCE:
Shevonne Bennett, Brown Sugar

'I researched a few estate agents, met up with a couple and saw about seven properties, but I knew I wanted a place in this area. Size was really important to me and when I walked into this place I connected with it straight away.'

LOCATION

Choosing a location for your restaurant involves far more than just picking a postcode. You will need to think long and hard, not just about the area you choose, but also the type of location. The first thing to decide on is whether your restaurant would be suited to the high street, a shopping centre or retail park or somewhere more tucked away.

The high street

An obvious choice due to the high levels of passing trade. You will be noticed
on the high street and therefore may not have to rely as much on advertising
or promotion. However, rents are high, property is harder to obtain and you will
need to be pitching to the same type of customers as other restaurants in the
area to succeed. You will also need to bear in mind what position you have on the
high street. Being located at the wrong end of the street, or even the wrong side
of the road can have a massive impact on trade.

Shopping centres and retail parks

Food outlets in retail areas have had something of a growth spurt over recent
years. Locating your restaurant in a shopping centre has its advantages. There
is plenty of passing trade, a captive audience even. Parking is also likely to be
easy for your customers as almost all shopping centres have their own car parks.
However, rent will be high, your restaurant will probably have to conform to the
type of outlet the shopping centre is looking for, and unless there's a cinema or
some other form of evening entertainment in the centre, you may find evening
trade is slow or even non-existent.

Tucked-away location

The obvious advantage to opening your restaurant somewhere less prominent
is cheaper property costs. More quiet secluded areas are also likely to attract

a different type of customer to that of the high street or retail park sites, and people will often travel longer distances and seek out hidden restaurants with a reputation for serving fine cuisine. However, if your business will rely on passing trade you may find it hard to pull in the customers. You will have to do far more promotion to inform customers of your presence if you want to attract more than just the local residents.

Once you have decided what kind of location you want for your restaurant there are plenty of other factors to consider:

- Parking – how easy is it for your customers to visit? Are there plenty of parking spots near by? You need it to be as easy as possible for customers to visit.
- Competition – what other restaurants are in the area? Are they attracting the same kind of clientele you are after? Positioning yourself alongside the competition can make it tough to win diners. However, being located within a cluster of restaurants means there will always be plenty of prospective diners choosing where they want to eat that night.
- Proximity to suppliers – you need to position your restaurant within easy reach of suppliers. Getting hold of the right stock is crucial and if your restaurant is out of the way, suppliers may be reluctant to deliver, especially at short notice.
- Proximity to staff – if you want to attract the right level of talent for your restaurant you will need to make sure the location is both accessible and attractive for your staff.

Lastly, when choosing your location, think about whether you like it. You will be spending an awful lot of time in it, particularly during the first few months. You need to be in an area that is accessible and agreeable to you too!

FROM THE EXPERTS:
Iqbal Wahhab, The Cinnamon Club and Roast

'With The Cinnamon Club there were 300 people bidding for that site and I had to convince them that I could deliver the goods over Conran, The Ivy and the rest of them. With the location for Roast it was another beauty parade – Caprice, Conran, Hakkasan. But there was no point putting a Wagamama or a Hakkasan here because Borough Market is all about celebrating British produce and what better way of celebrating that than a restaurant that serves traditional British cooking?'

➡ COMMERCIAL CLASSIFICATION

Before you negotiate the lease or purchase of a property you must check what commercial classification it currently falls under. If the property does not already have the correct classification for a restaurant you need to get planning permission from your local authority. You must bear in mind that planning consent might not be accepted if the local authority feels the change of classification would not benefit the area.

When making a decision, the local authority will take into consideration factors such as whether there is a need for that type of business in the area, traffic and parking requirements, likely causes of nuisance such as noise, smells or environmental hazards the business may cause, trading hours and objections from other occupiers and residents.

There are five types of classification which the local authorities use to make sure there is an adequate balance of different types of commercial property in any one area. Businesses such as shops, hairdressing salons, post offices and travel agents fall under the A1 classification. A2 is reserved for professional and financial services such as banks, solicitors estate agents etc.

For your restaurant you must make sure your property has the A3 classification, which is often the hardest classification to obtain. You will find this also has a bearing on the rental or purchase value of your chosen premises. Simply put, premises with the A3 classification cost more.

Up until 2005 the A3 classification covered all food and drink establishments including restaurants, bars, pubs and takeaways. However, in April 2005 the classification was split and is now as follows:

- A3 – restaurants, snack bars and cafés
- A4 – pubs and bars
- A5 – takeaways

This means if you ever decided to change your A3 classified premises from a restaurant to a pub or takeaway you would need planning consent. However, changes from pub or takeaway to restaurant do not need prior consent as long as the permitted development rights have not been excluded in relation to your specific property.

➡ LEASE OR BUY

You may not be in a position to even choose whether you rent or buy your business property. If you don't have the capital to put towards buying a property, you'll be left with the option of renting. However, even if buying is a financial option, you should still weigh up the pros and cons of buying or renting first.

Buying

For many budding restaurateurs, the idea of owning your own property is just too much of a pipe dream. Property is expensive and, with so many costs involved in setting up a new business, a mortgage is an avoidable one.

Ask yourself the following questions before you decide to buy a property. If you can't answer yes to all of them, buying isn't for you.

- Is the restaurant in the best location you think you can ever afford?
- Do you plan to keep your restaurant the same size indefinitely?
- Do you have either a sufficient deposit and the budget for a mortgage, or enough cash to purchase the property outright?

If you're in a comfortable enough position to buy your restaurant premises, then there are several advantages associated with buying a property. The first and most obvious is that you'll own it, have the freedom do with it as you please, and not have to answer to a landlord. Another major advantage with owning your own restaurant premises is you'll have a major asset, either to secure loans against or think of as an investment.

IN MY EXPERIENCE:
Lisa Tse, Sweet Mandarin

'It took us over a year to find the right spot for our restaurant. We eventually found it through a surveyor who said the area was really going places. We'd always had the intention of building the restaurant from scratch because it was like a blank canvas. We could come in and build whatever specification we needed. We didn't want to buy someone else's goodwill because it was dead money to us. We saw it as an investment deal too, and knew that if the business didn't work in that area we would have an exit strategy.'

As with any property purchase, domestic or commercial, you'll need to carry out the appropriate checks before you agree to buy. Bring in a reputable surveyor, get the place checked with the environmental health officer and find out what your business rates will be. Do as much research on the building and area as physically possible because if something's not right with it once you've got the keys, it won't be easy to just pack up and move on.

Leasing

Leasing is far more common than buying, for the simple reason that it gives you more flexibility in both a physical and a financial sense. If you expand more quickly than anticipated, you can move at relatively short-notice provided you negotiated the right kind of contract when you took out the lease. Also, there are a limited number of properties on the market to buy and you'll find your options are far more open when looking for leased property.

A lease can be negotiated for any length of time that you and the landlord agree on, but typically will last anywhere between 3–25 years. The landlord will be looking for a reliable tenant that will run a successful business and consequently be able to pay the rent on time. You may be asked to present a business plan and have your own financial history checked up on. If you don't have any trading history then it's not unheard of for the landlord to ask for anything up to a year's rent in advance, so bear this in mind when budgeting.

However, you have just as much right to do your own checks on the landlord. If possible talk to the current or previous tenants. Find out why they're moving on. If their business failed was it because of the location, something wrong with the property, or even as a result of a difficult landlord? These are the kind of things you'll want to know before signing a lease.

IN MY EXPERIENCE:
Eza Philippe Navaratnasingam, The Lounge

'I found our property through an estate agent after searching online, but it was nine months later before we actually moved in. There were a lot of issues with the landlord and I had to get a solicitor friend to help me out. The lease was a lot of trouble to get transferred. Documents kept getting held up between the different parties, and it just took so long for everything to move forward.'

It's easy to get burned when it comes to property deals and the best way to protect yourself is to ask all the right questions, get everything agreed in writing and above all, check your contract with a fine toothcomb. Here are a few tips and things to consider before signing a lease:

- What kind of rent are similar businesses in the area being charged, and is yours a fare rate in comparison?
- Is the length of lease suitable? If it's too short your restaurant will lack security, but if it's too long and you don't have a break clause, you may find yourself stuck.
- Is the building sound and in a state of good repair? It's advisable to bring in expert help to check there are no serious faults.
- Will the landlord offer a rent-free period if there are repairs to be carried out?
- Do you need planning permission before you can build or alter the restaurant according to your designs?
- Who is responsible for insurance? What's included in the rent, and what cover will the landlord expect you to take out yourself in addition?

This is by no means an extensive list of everything you should check before signing a contract. It's always advisable to have a solicitor or property expert to check over the small print for you.

➡ PROFESSIONAL ADVISORS

Estate agents

These guys often get a rough deal reputation-wise, but if you find an agent or company that are helpful and trustworthy then that's half the battle won. Having said that, it's always a good idea to shop around. With the internet at your fingertips you can search for properties that suit your requirements and rule out ones that don't, without having to listen to a sales pitch.

Once you've got yourself on a few estate agents' books, speak to them regularly. Make sure they know exactly what you're looking for so they don't waste your valuable time by showing you round unsuitable properties

Helpful estate agents can also do more for you than put you in contact with landlords and property owners. An estate agent that specialises in commercial property may be able to put you in touch with other professional advisors such as architects, surveyors and solicitors.

IN MY EXPERIENCE:

Shevonne Bennett, Brown Sugar

'I approached a couple of solicitors through my estate agent and they helped me a lot. They really filled in the gaps in my knowledge and even got me some compensation from my landlord for delays.'

Solicitors

Getting the right help on board is essential. It's better to have someone steering you clear of problems rather than hiring them to put out fires further down the line. As mentioned, it's really not advisable to sign any contract without it being looked over by an independent legal expert in the property sector.

If possible, get someone on board who specialises in the restaurant trade. If they've overseen countless restaurant sales and leases in the past, the chances are they'll spot any problems or concerns with your deal a mile away. To find a specialised solicitor why not try The Law Society. You can search by location or sector at www.lawsociety.org.uk

Builders and architects

IN MY EXPERIENCE:

Lisa Tse, Sweet Mandarin

'We were fortunate and found an architect who'd already done a project we all really liked. It all started with a chat in a coffee bar. He then helped us get the team together and do the step-by-step project plans. It was by no means easy because we had so many problems during the four weeks of building, but he really helped.'

Choosing an architect or builder that comes highly recommended is the best way to find someone trustworthy and capable of doing a satisfactory job. Go through organisations such as the Federation of Master Builders (www.fmb.org.uk). Ask friends or other restaurateurs for advice, or ask for examples of previous work so you can see for yourself what the finished results look like.

FROM THE EXPERTS:
Simon Kossoff, Carluccio's

'I'd been working as a consultant at the time of raising funding and had a lot of contacts in the industry. We somehow found ourselves in the fortuitous position of having the property if we raised the money and not being committed to it if we didn't. I'm not quite sure how we did it and I've never been in same position since. We signed the contract for the money on the Friday and the builders started work the following Monday. It took us 16 weeks to build the first restaurant. We now do it in half that time.'

You may not be an expert when it comes to building terms, how long things take or how much it's all likely to cost, but it's up to you to do your research and arm yourself with as much knowledge as possible. The more you know, the less likely you are to be taken advantage of.

FROM THE EXPERTS:
Iqbal Wahhab, The Cinnamon Club, Roast

'I had to learn so many things I'd had no idea I'd need to with The Cinnamon Club. I'd sit around in meetings with architects, engineers and builders and not have a clue what they were on about. I'd just sign it all off until we got to the point where we'd completely run out of money. It got to the stage where the builders were walking off, so I had to go out and raise more cash. With Roast I made sure I knew what I was talking about and would chair the builders' meetings. I became an expert on draining and plumbing! I wasn't going to let anyone pull the wool over my eyes this time, so even though it was tedious and unglamorous, I learned it all.'

Before you sign a lease or agree to a mortgage, make sure you've considered all of the following:

- Have other restaurants been successful in the premises? If not, why not? Can you succeed where they've failed?
- Is it the right size? Can you seat enough diners and have a big enough kitchen to meet the projections in your business plan?
- Does the kitchen meet the required standards for food hygiene as well as heath and safety? Has the environmental health officer given it the thumbs up?
- Is the property security friendly? Is it easy to break into? Does it have a burglar alarm, and if not, how much would it cost to add one?
- Are there any major structural problems or damaged areas?
- How much are you likely to pay in business rates?
- Are you really certain it's the best possible place for you to locate your restaurant?

Things to remember:

- Consider your property needs carefully before you even start viewing properties. You need a clear idea of exactly what you require before speaking to agents.

- Weigh up the different options for locations.

- Remember to check the commercial classification of any property you're interested in.

- Don't rush into buying if leasing is more suited to your finances.

- Find a solicitor and estate agent you feel comfortable with.

Martin Felstead, Managing Director of Aspen Design, explains that there are many considerations to take into account when equipping a restaurant for the first time:

1. Check where your main services are located

Firstly, find out the position of the main services such as drains, water, gas and electricity, for these will govern where certain items of equipment have to be located. It is also important to work out how and where the extraction system will conduct grease and fumes to atmosphere. In an existing premises you may have to work with what you've inherited, but it is always worth considering whether it might be more economical in the long run to have things moved.

2. Evaluate your space

Next, you need to look at the available space. A common mistake among new operators is to forget all the extras that might be needed, such as a dry store, cold room, COSH store, changing room and, in larger establishments, a chef's office. Make sure you factor everything you need into your plan.

The fabric of the kitchen will also need to be considered, to ensure that whatever is going to be covering the walls, floor and ceiling is both easy to clean and conforms with Health & Safety regulations.

3. Kitting out the kitchen

Only then can you start to look at your menus, and at the number of people you will be feeding, in order to determine the kitchen equipment required. If your kitchen is small, it may well be that you need to purchase items of a higher spec to ensure that you gain maximum efficiency coupled with minimum power usage. A lot will also depend on what you can afford, but it is a common mistake to trawl internet sites such as eBay in the hope of securing a real bargain. In truth, such bargains are rare, and you do not want to be landed with something that is cheap and flimsy, cannot do the job it's supposed to do and comes with no warranty or guarantee.

4. The aesthetics

Once you have considered all of the above, you'll be ready to embark on the design. Don't just think about what looks good: it is crucial to ensure that there is ease of use, that work flows are good, and that your staff will be safe when they're working for you.

Many people are afraid to seek professional help for fear that it will cost them dear. Of course, the services of a catering consultant don't come cheap, but many kitchen design and supply companies will offer free advice and an initial design free of charge, so it is always worth asking. To talk to Aspen Design about your new business, call FREE on **0800 389 1546**.

Decking it out

Y ou've signed the lease and collected the keys, but what comes next? Now comes the exciting but gruelling task of getting your restaurant ready to open. Whether you've gone for a fully operational kitchen and dining area, or have chosen to build up your restaurant from scratch, you need to consider all your options carefully.

Again there are some vital matters you need to consider before you start choosing your tableware. Issues such as environmental health requirements and utilities are covered here as well as advice on designing the optimum layout for your restaurant, both for the kitchen and the dining area. This chapter also covers the essential equipment you'll need to get your restaurant up and running, such as kitchen utensils, tablecloths and tills for the front of house.

In this chapter we'll cover:

- Things to consider before you start
- Dealing with contractors
- Décor
- Layout
- Signage
- Equipment

➡ BEFORE YOU PICK UP A PAINTBRUSH . . .

Your best planning skills are needed for this stage of the setting up process.
Every aspect of the restaurant's physical appearance and functionality has to be
thought out before you start drilling into walls or choosing cookers.

Environmental health officer

If you haven't done so already, it's a good idea at this stage to bring in an
environmental health officer to talk you through what you need to do to meet
legal requirements for your restaurant. It's better to find out now if you need

specific pest control measures, or your
design plan doesn't allow for adequate
separation between raw and cooked
food preparation areas. Contact
your local council for details of your
environmental health department.

> **TIP**
>
> Bringing an expert in during
> the planning stage could end up
> saving you thousands of pounds and
> even prevent delays in opening.

Utilities

Another area to think through carefully is utilities. It's tempting to leave things
as they are if the premises already has gas and electricity set up, but the current
suppliers may not be the most cost-effective for your business. Shop around and
get the best deal. A few hours invested in comparing gas and electricity prices
may save you a considerable amount in the long-run.

 IN MY EXPERIENCE:
Shevonne Bennett, Brown Sugar

'When I arrived on the first day the place was a complete tip and I had to start from
scratch. There was no gas and no electricity. I don't know why but I just expected it
all to be working!'

> ### ⚓ TIP
> Find out from your landlord or the previous premises owner what the situation is for running water, gas and electricity before you get the keys. You won't be able to do much without working utilities and it may be something you can sort out before the handover of the restaurant.

DIY or contractors?

Your business plan should have already helped you decide whether or not you'll be doing a DIY job or hiring professional decorators, architects or builders. Even if you decide to do the work yourself, it's a good idea to get some professional advice before you start as they may point out some issues you hadn't considered.

If you decide to bring in contractors you need to have thought about the following before choosing who you want to build your restaurant:

- The kind of atmosphere you want to achieve
- The colour scheme/design theme you're leaning towards
- The layout of both the kitchen and dining area
- The price you're prepared to pay

You need to have thought all of the above through before the first contractor walks through the door so that you can give them a true idea of what they need to offer you, and to avoid being taken advantage of. Don't accept the first price and package you're offered. Get as many different quotations and pitches as time will allow for then compare them before you make a decision. The last thing you need is trouble with your builders or designers, as this is the most likely cause of a delay in opening or going over budget. For extra reassurance it's worth going via trade bodies such as the Federation of Master Builders. It may cost more, but at least then you can be more confident of a professional service.

Timing

Unfortunately delays are common when it comes to getting a restaurant ready for to launch. When planning your opening you might want to consider budgeting in time for unexpected delays. Of course, you can't foresee every problem, but preparing yourself for the odd setback can take some of the pressure off if you do run into roadblocks.

IN MY EXPERIENCE:

Ian Pengelley, Gilgamesh

'Every successful project looks like a disaster in the middle. Things go wrong with openings and you've got to be able to deal with it. You need to be flexible, because restaurants never open on time. There's always going to be issues with building and staffing so rather than just shout and lose your temper, you've got to work out how to move things forward.'

➡ RESTAURANT LAYOUT

How you arrange your kitchen and dining area has a significant impact on how you run your restaurant. Something as simple as a slightly narrow corridor between the kitchen and dining room could prove disastrous on a busy night as waiters get under each other's feet. However, it's not just a question of cramped spaces making it hard for staff to move around. If your kitchen doesn't have adequate space to separate raw and cooked foods for example, you may be in breach of food safety requirements.

When viewing properties you should take the layout into careful consideration and try to imagine your kitchen fully staffed and a bustling dining room decked out with tables, chairs and a lot of hungry customers. You'll also need to give careful consideration to areas such as an office (if you require one), the stock room and food storage areas as well as customer and staff toilet facilities.

Kitchens

How many different sections or areas your kitchen is divided into will be dependent on its size, and the kind of food you serve. Whatever size kitchen you have however, it needs to have the following four areas clearly distinguished:

- Cold preparation
- Cooking area
- Dishwashing area
- Storage area

Larger kitchens will have divisions within these four areas including a service area where the chefs place the food before the waiter picks it up and several different preparation areas where meat, poultry fish and vegetables are kept apart.

IN MY EXPERIENCE:
Eza Philippe Navaratnasingam, The Lounge

'The kitchen took about six months to get exactly how I wanted it. It was such a big job that when we first opened we mainly just operated as a bar because we didn't have the right facilities. It was two years before I had a good enough extractor, which I ended up building myself because contractors were quoting such high prices.'

Take advice from an environmental health officer before starting any work on a new kitchen. If you're moving into an already fully operational kitchen then make sure it conforms to basic food hygiene standards. Pest control measures you need to be aware of include making sure waste storage areas aren't attracting unwanted visitors, and there are no entry routes into your kitchen. You'll also need to ensure any kitchen windows have netting fitted to prevent insects flying in.

Further, you'll need to make sure every aspect of the kitchen layout is convenient. Your storage area must be easily accessible and in a suitable place for deliveries to be stored away, and simultaneously easy enough for chefs to access during the middle of a service.

IN MY EXPERIENCE:

Ian Pengelley, Gilgamesh

'The original kitchen designers for Gilgamesh were horrendous. I had to build around it. Our restaurant is very much design-orientated so we had a lot of building problems. At first we had our washing-up area downstairs so all the plates had to be taken down to be washed then brought back up again. I ended up having to build a washing-up area outside at the back of the kitchen.'

Dining area

Your tables should be arranged to strike a balance between being able to seat the right number of covers in each service, easy access for waiters and adequate space between diners.

You'll also need a range of different sized tables to seat the variations in party size of your diners. Try to make tables easy to cluster. If a large party comes in during a busy service, you'll want them to be seated as quickly and effortlessly as a possible. Bear in mind that square tables are far easier to rearrange for larger party sizes.

Think about the best place to position the bar in terms how you'll arrange the tables. In a small premises you need to be as economical with your space as possible, so counters, the types of chairs you use and even the shape of your tables can effect how many covers you can seat at any one time.

Try to avoid positioning tables too close to the entrance of the restaurant as diners often get frustrated with the constant entry of other customers, especially if people are hanging around waiting to be seated. Likewise, a table too close to the kitchen entrance can be inconvenient and may block the path of your waiting staff.

If you've got a large dining area, why not try breaking up the space with tall plants? It may add to the atmosphere, and give your customers some privacy from each other.

 # DESIGN

A growing number of modern restaurants attract diners just as much, if not more, because of design than the food they serve. The look and feel of restaurant will determine the type of customers you attract, and the type of occasion they choose to visit your establishment for.

Restaurant design involves far more than the colour you choose to paint the walls. It's everything from the plates you serve you food on, to the sinks you install in the bathroom; the uniforms your staff wear to the font you use on your menus.

Colour

Relate colour to the type of food you're serving and the kind of atmosphere you want to achieve. In crude terms, reds and oranges would create a lively and bustling restaurant, and blues and greens work for more relaxed establishments.

Avoid garish colours unless you're trying to make a particular impact on your customers. However, likewise too much white or cream can make people feel they're in a canteen or dining hall.

If you've got a very small dining area avoid colours that are too dark on the walls as this may make the room feel even more cramped. Don't forget that plainer walls can be complemented with brighter or stronger colours in other areas such as furniture, tableware or upholstery.

IN MY EXPERIENCE:
Shevonne Bennett, Brown Sugar

'When I started Brown Sugar, I knew I wanted a really modern feel. Browns and creams were really in fashion at the time and they suited my ideas for the restaurant theme perfectly.'

Furniture

Before you buy your furniture it's important to strike a balance between what you want design-wise, and what's suitable and functional for your restaurant. Think about comfort, shape, durability and cost.

Furniture buying is one area you can save money without compromising on quality or style. Buying second-hand may give you a better class of furniture for your money and may even fit in with your design theme.

If you're going for static furniture such as in-built booths make sure you shop around when it comes to designers and carpenters. It's always worth getting more than one opinion or quote for the work.

IN MY EXPERIENCE:

Eza Philippe Navaratnasingam, The Lounge

'When we moved into the premises I kept the original tables but eventually got some second-hand chapel chairs. We also changed our signage to be clearer and more effective. With the old sign people weren't quite sure what kind of place we were, but once we spelled it out – The Lounge Spanish Tapas Bar – turnover and food sales really started going up.'

Signage

Like so much talked about in this chapter, your signage is wholly dependent on the kind of look and feel you want for your restaurant. Try not to waste money on extravagantly lit signs and lettering outside your restaurant unless it really suits the type of establishment you're running.

Sandwich boards can work well outside if you want to inform passing potential customers of offers or specials on the menu. Be careful of spelling mistakes though, and make sure you've included any exclusions or exceptions when advertising special offers.

Design for signage should match up with the choices you made when considering the identity and the name of your business. Go back to section one for help on this.

Toilets

Some restaurants make their toilets a real talking point. Funky tile designs or extravagant sinks can make your restaurant really memorable. The main thing to remember is: don't go beyond your means. If you don't have the time or money to maintain an extravagant restroom area then keep it simple and easy to clean.

Throughout a service make sure the toilets are kept clean and well stocked with soap, toilet paper and hand drying facilities. You'll also need to make sure locks and doors are in good working order at all times, or you may have some flustered and irate customers on your hands. Toilets should be checked throughout each service to make sure there are no nasty surprises awaiting customers. A good rule is to get one of your waiting staff or porters to have a quick check once an hour.

Toilets should also be of sufficient distance from the kitchen, and the door to a lavatory must not open directly onto food preparation areas. You should also have separate hand washing facilities for your staff as they should not be using the same sinks that are used to wash food.

Equipment

Think carefully about the equipment you need. You don't want to be overstretched when it comes to having enough cutlery or chinaware, but at the same time, if you don't get your estimates right you may end up over-buying.

The same goes for kitchen equipment. Think about what you actually need to make the type of food on you menu, and avoid buying unnecessary contraptions which you think might come in useful at some point.

TIP

Be economical but don't go for the cheapest options on the market. The old adage 'you buy cheap, you buy twice' certainly rings true when it comes to kitchenware, and you might end up spending more in the long run if the equipment isn't up to scratch.

Buying second-hand or leasing equipment is a good way to save money during the early stages of your business without compromising on quality. There are plenty of companies online and in business directories that will lease you equipment, allowing you to work out what you use most, and what apparatus you think you should return.

As mentioned, your specific requirements will depend upon the type of restaurant you're running and the style of food you serve, but as a general rule, you'll need the following heavy duty pieces of equipment, all of which can be purchased second-hand or leased if you're on a tight budget:

- Six-burner gas stove with double oven
- Deep fat-fryer
- Grill
- Ice machine
- Commercial dishwasher and possibly separate glass washer
- Espresso/coffee maker
- Large commercial fridge and separate freezer

There are a hundred and one other kitchen items you'll need, from cheese graters to spatulas, but the list will vary depending on the size and style of your kitchen. Again don't go for the cheapest items as you'll probably spend more replacing them a couple of months down the line.

Some tips to bear in mind when buying smaller items for your restaurant:

- Choose plates, glasses and cutlery than can be easily replaced with matching items. Breakages and losses will occur, and you'll want to find the same designs again rather than replacing your entire stock.
- Ask your drinks suppliers what they can provide you with before you buy items such as glasses. They may kit your bar out for free depending on what kind of deal you sign with them.
- Avoid cheap linens that don't stand up to very hot washes. Wine and food stains will take their toll and you can't afford to use new ones every service.
- You'll need a good range of kitchen knives, but professional chefs will often prefer to use their own or have a preference for a certain type. Discuss this with your chef before you splash out.

The little bits that add up (use the following as an absolute minimum):

Front of house

- Table cloths – 5 per table
- Napkins – 10 per diner space
- Small flower vases – use ratio of 1 per table with 1 spare for every 5 tables
- Salt and pepper pots – same ratio as vases

- Knives, forks and dessert spoons – 10 per diner space
- Soup spoons – 10 per diner space
- Tea spoons – 10 per diner space
- Side plates – 10 per diner space
- Large plates – 12 per diner space
- Wine glasses – 15 per diner space (you need to buy in larger quantities to account for breakages)
- Tumblers – 15 per diner space
- Champagne flutes – 5 per diner space
- Water jugs – 3 per table
- Corkscrew – 1 per waiter and barman
- Bread basket – 3 per table
- Coffee cups – 4 per diner space

Back of house

- Grater
- Fruit corer
- Spatulas
- Roasting and baking trays
- Measuring jug
- Ladles
- Mixing spoons
- Sieve
- Colander
- Cast iron pans
- Mixing bowls
- Coloured chopping boards for veg, dairy, fish and raw meat
- Kitchen knives (discuss with chef)
- Lemon squeezer and zester
- Funnel
- Tongs
- Balloon whisk
- Potato masher

IN MY EXPERIENCE:

Shevonne Bennett, Brown Sugar

'You can get a lot of staff training free from drinks companies. They provide you with so much more than you imagine. They'll do drinks menus for you, give you free items such as glasses, cocktail shakers and umbrellas. When I started I bought a lot of stuff that I didn't need to simply because I didn't know what I could get for free. There are a lot of freebies out there. You just have to be confident and demand a bit more.'

Tills

You will need at least one till for your restaurant depending on its size and scale of operation. Smaller establishments can get away with a basic system, while more complicated operations will want to go with a more advanced electronic point of sale (EPoS) system. This is another area where you can choose to either lease or buy.

The more sophisticated EPoS systems will have computerised touch screens which can keep track of exactly what's been ordered and give you accurate up-to-date figures on what your most popular dishes and drinks are. However the cost of these can run into the thousands and you may find that a standalone system which provides paper printouts is more than adequate for your operation.

For details on how to apply for merchant status to receive credit card payments see the *Getting legal* chapter.

Security

Now that you've started to kit out your restaurant with equipment, you need to make sure it's secure. Don't try and save money when it comes to locks, bolts and secure doors and windows. If it doesn't look impenetrable it'll just attract thieves. An alarm is a must, and preferably one that alerts a security company rather than just making a loud noise. You'll pay a monthly fee of at least £40–£50 for this service but it'll be well worth it for the peace of mind. Think about the last time you heard an alarm going off. Did you bother to check out the problem or alert the authorities? Don't rely on other people to take notice when it's your restaurant under threat.

Things to remember:

- Consult an environmental health officer. It could save you a lot of time and money, not to mention prevent you from having to correct mistakes down the line.

- Check your utilities are due to work before you move in. You may arrive to a gasless, electricity-free property.

- Don't be tempted to decorate solely to your taste. It's your customers that need to feel the most comfortable.

- Consider leasing equipment as a way to free up cashflow during your first few months.

You have carefully selected the location of your restaurant, chosen the furniture and planned the décor to reflect your desired image. After all, creating an atmosphere for your customer to enjoy is vital. Music plays an integral role in this and should be carefully considered as part of your business plan.

How can music benefit my restaurant?

- Music can help to create your desired image and to attract the right type of clientele to your restaurant. Think about your customers and the music they would expect to hear.
- Music can create ambience, making your restaurant a welcoming and interesting place and helping you to stand out from your competitors.
- Live music, even a small band once a month, can really bring in the crowds and help increase takings.
- Music can mask private conversations, putting your customers at ease.
- Music can improve staff motivation, performance and morale, helping to increase staff and customer satisfaction.

In order to reap the benefits of using music in your restaurant, you legally require a PRS Music Licence.

Why do I need a PRS Music Licence?

Under the Copyright Designs and Patents Act 1988, when a song or a piece of music is written, the person who wrote it owns the copyright and has the right to decide how and when it should be played. PRS was set up by songwriters, composers and music publishers to manage these rights on their behalf. This means that a PRS Music Licence grants you the legal permission to play millions of songs.

Do I need a PRS Music Licence to play music from overseas?

PRS have agreements with societies all over the world so no matter where the music you want to play originates from, a PRS Music Licence is legally required.

Where does my money go?

The money collected from PRS Music Licences is distributed to the writers and composers of music from around the world and is essential in supporting them while they create more music.

For more information about PRS and to view case studies and research about the benefits that music can bring to your restaurant, please visit us at **www.prs.co.uk**

To buy a PRS Music Licence please call us on **0800 068 4828**.

T o run a safe and legal business there are a whole plethora of laws and regulations you must abide by. You can't afford to let any of these obligations slide when you run a food business or you could find yourself in some serious hot water.

This chapter will lead you through all of the requirements you need to meet in order to run your restaurant legally. These requirements cover issues such as payment and how to obtain merchant status so you can accept credit card payments, as well as your obligation as a business owner to watch out for counterfeit notes when taking cash payments. We also cover the kinds of insurance you will need to protect your customers, your staff and your business should anything go wrong.

Be sure to read the section on legal issues specific to restaurants, such as environmental health visits and licensing laws to ensure your restaurant is up to code.

In this chapter we'll cover:

- Money and credit cards
- Insurance
- The smoking ban
- Licensing

- Environmental health
- Food hygiene
- Health and safety

➡ MONEY

Credit cards

Getting merchant status is necessary if you want to accept credit and debit card payments in your restaurant. Even today, there are still some smaller cafés and restaurants that get by only accepting cash and cheques but to make life easier for your customers you probably won't want to rely solely on this type of payment.

> ### ✦ TIP
> It's really important you get your merchant status sorted out as quickly as you can. Customers are put off by the inconvenience, and not being able to pay with a card can be a real pain. Only accepting cash will certainly save you on card processing fees but you could lose far more by customers choosing the restaurants next door if they don't have cash on them.

When applying for merchant status you'll be subject to some stringent security checks. Even without trading history you can still apply. However, acceptance is not automatic. High levels of fraud mean that credit card companies use various methods to ensure illegal activity is kept to a minimum.

One of these methods is chargebacks. If a charge is found to be fraudulent, the money paid by the credit card company can be taken back from you. This can occur up to six months after the transaction has taken place and it then becomes up to you to recover the fraudulent funds.

The point is, since you can be held responsible for any fraudulent use of cards in your restaurant, the banks need to know you will take adequate measures to prevent it.

The process of applying for merchant status involves getting in touch with your bank. The main high street banks offer more or less the same uniform services. The process takes about a fortnight and as previously mentioned, new businesses do not generally have to prove trading history. However, new businesses will be asked to provide their business plans. Longer established restaurants will generally have to produce around three years' worth of accounts. If you plan to take any food orders over the phone you'll need to state this at the time of applying, as 'customer not present' transactions require special permission.

In terms of price, it's a good idea to shop around if you are willing to look further afield than your business bank account provider. Most of the main banks charge roughly 3% per transaction, £15–£25 per month for the rental of the swipe machine and a one-off set up fee of £100–£150.

So that's the average cost, however you can get these prices down with the right kind of negotiation. Don't be afraid to ask for a lower rate. The worst-case scenario is the bank saying no.

Cash forgery

Despite the dramatic increase in paying with plastic over the last couple of decades, restaurants still accept a lot of cash. You therefore must be aware of the forgery risks. Counterfeit notes are still relatively rare, but it pays to educate yourself on how to recognise a fake.

Knowingly accepting fake notes is clearly illegal, however you're also responsible for making sure any cash you accept is genuine. Ignorance is not an excuse so you can't just turn a blind eye if you suspect customers have given you counterfeit money. Banks will not accept fake notes from you so you will lose out financially if you don't apply an adequate level of vigilance.

When checking for fake notes, don't just rely on one method. Feel the notes in your hands and if in doubt, compare with one you know is genuine. The easiest way to check notes are genuine is with an ultra violet pen. The pen causes a chemical reaction between the ink and the paper, but you'll need to replace them regularly as dirty pens can be unreliable.

> If you don't have any kind of counterfeit-detecting device a few elements to use to determine genuine notes to are:
>
> - The paper and raised print
> - The metallic thread
> - The watermark
> - The print quality
> - The hologram

If you suspect you have received a counterfeit note you must report it to the police immediately. They will then give you a receipt and send it to the Bank of

England. If it turns out to be genuine, they will refund you. For more information visit www.bankofengland.co.uk.

Refunds

Customers eating in your restaurant have the right to a certain standard of food and service. The law does give them the right to demand a refund or allow them to refuse payment in certain circumstances.

Under the Trade Descriptions Act the food your menu describes must be an accurate reflection of the food you serve. This includes wine lists, ingredients, and descriptions involving the manner in which the food was cooked. For example, if you claim the food is 'home-made' and it's not, you are breaking the law.

Under the Supply of Goods Act you must also provide food of adequate quality. If you serve something below this standard, the customer is within his or her right to ask for a replacement or refuse to pay for it. They do not, however, have the right to refuse to pay the entire bill, only the cost of the offending dish.

It makes no difference if the customer has partly consumed or completely finished their meal, they still have the same rights under the aforementioned acts. There's more on dealing with unhappy customers in *Surviving the First Six Months*.

➡ INSURANCE

At this stage in the life of your restaurant you probably won't want to think about all the things that can go wrong, but making sure you have the right level of insurance cover is an absolute necessity. Some types of insurance are required by law, while others are not compulsory but are essential if you want to protect your business against every eventuality.

Employers Liability Insurance (ELI)

If you employ even a single other member of staff you are required by law to have this cover, or you could face a fine. This type of insurance helps employers meet the cost of compensation for staff if they are injured while working. Policies generally start at around £10m worth of cover to include legal expenses. However,

ELI doesn't mean you're untouchable. You must still honour all your health and safety obligations, carry out regular risk assessments and have all the appropriate paperwork to back this up.

Product and public liability insurance

Although not compulsory by law, as a restaurateur you'd be very foolish not to take out this kind of cover. By taking out this cover you will be insured against claims made against your restaurant by members of the public. As your business relies on members of the public entering your premises and eating the food you produce, you need to protect yourself should anything untoward happen. However, you still have to make sure the food you serve meets certain quality standards, otherwise your claim is likely to be unsuccessful.

Premises insurance

Your restaurant's chance of survival will be severely compromised if the actual premises is damaged. You need to be covered against damage as a result of any number of unforeseen occurrences such as floods, fires, or malicious damage. If your premises is rented, you may not be responsible for taking out this cover, but if that is the case, you'll want to make sure your landlord has taken care of it. Tenants are generally always responsible for shop fronts however.

Contents insurance

As premises insurance only covers the physical building, you'll need to make sure the contents of your restaurant are also adequately insured against damage or theft. This will cover stock, machinery, restaurant furniture and anything else included in the policy.

Business interruption insurance

While covering you against the costs of repair and replacement, contents and premises insurance won't necessarily help with any income you lose while your

restaurant is closed as a result of unforeseen events. This is where business interruption insurance comes in.

➡ RESTAURANT-SPECIFIC LAW

The legal requirements we've covered so far apply to most businesses. However, there is plenty of legislation which applies specifically to the hospitality trade. Before you open the doors to the first customer make sure you've covered ALL of the following regulations.

Smoking

In July 2007, a smoking ban was introduced in England, having already been established in Scotland, Wales and Northern Ireland. The ban made smoking in all enclosed public spaces and workplaces illegal.

Under no circumstances can you allow customers or staff to smoke inside your restaurant. The smoking ban also extends to any company vehicles used by more than one person. The ban is enforced by local authorities and failure to adhere to it carries a fine of up to £2,500.

Noise control

Successful restaurants are by their very nature bustling, and with that inevitably comes a certain amount of noise. However, it's your responsibility as a restaurateur to make sure the noise level of your establishment does not exceed what's acceptable.

Under environment legislation, if noise from your restaurant has a negative impact on the public, which includes nearby residents, you can be found guilty of causing a statutory nuisance.

If a complaint is lodged against your business, the local authority can serve you with an abatement notice

> ### ✦ TIP
> For more advice on your responsibilities towards keeping local residents happy, contact your local authority for some advice. You can find a list of all local councils at www.direct.gov.uk.

ordering you to reduce or stop any noise. Of course, the type of restaurant you run will determine how noisy an establishment it's likely to be. However, if you are planning on it being a fairly lively establishment, you might want to consider non-residential locations for it.

Licensing

The Licensing Act 2003, which came into force in England and Wales in November 2005, requires businesses to have a licence if they wish to sell or supply alcohol or sell hot food or drink between 11pm and 5am. Even if your restaurant does not serve alcohol, you'll need to close before 11pm to avoid the need for a licence.

Under the new system, you apply to your local authority for a single licence to carry out any or all of these activities. The new single licence can also incorporate public entertainment licences which would include, for example, things like live music.

When applying for a new licence, or to change or add to your licence, you need to let other residents and local businesses know your intentions. You do this by putting up a notice on the premises for 28 days and by placing an advertisement in a local paper or circular. You also need to notify the police and environmental health service.

To serve alcohol in your restaurant you need to appoint a personal licence holder who will be named on the licence. Depending on what is stipulated in your licence you may not need to apply for further permission for certain entertainment events at your restaurant. If you are unsure, contact your local authority who will inform you of your legal requirements.

Health and safety

Running a restaurant business involves employing staff and inviting members of the public onto your premises. You must therefore make sure you implement adequate health and safety practices from the outset. This can involve a lot of tedious paperwork, and laborious training, but unfortunately there's just no getting away from it.

You are responsible for the wellbeing of every single person affected by your restaurant. These people include:

- Staff
- Customers
- Any visitors to your premises, from the delivery people to the plumber

Accidents and injuries are more likely to occur in a kitchen than in an office or shop. When staff are dealing with open flames and knives on a daily basis, the odd minor injury such as a cut or burn is practically inevitable. However, you need to make sure you have taken all the necessary precautions and implemented procedures to minimise these risks and deal with them as quickly and effectively as possible when they do occur.

Before you or your staff start working in the restaurant you should conduct an assessment of the health and safety risks your businesses faces. You are required to have a formal policy based on this assessment. If you employ five or more people then this policy must be written down.

As an employer, your legal requirements surrounding health and safety are as follows. You should:

- Record and report all accidents
- Consult all staff on health and safety measures
- Ensure staff are aware of health and safety procedures and comply with them

Your local authority and the Health and Safety Executive (HSE) are the governing bodies that make sure you are meeting your obligations. However, they are not just there to enforce and punish you when you make a mistake. You can also ask their advice and even invite them to your restaurant premises to help you with your risk assessment and safety procedures.

 TIP

For more information on health and safety and how to carry out a risk assessment of your business you can visit the HSE website at www.hse.gov.uk.

Environmental health visits

It's a good idea to get a consultation from an environmental health officer before you agree on a specific property, as if the premises doesn't meet basic standards you will not be permitted to trade. However, if you decide on a property before you've spoken to an officer you must still register your premises with the local authority at least 28 days before opening your restaurant. You are then subject to inspections every six months, although depending on your local authority it may not be as frequent as this.

There are a number of reasons why an environmental health officer may decide to call on your restaurant out of the blue. It could simply be a routine inspection, or perhaps in response to a reported accident or complaint.

Officers are permitted by law to enter commercial premises at any reasonable time. They are also allowed to bring assistance such as in the form of a tradesperson or police officer.

Environmental officers have the right to demand all relevant information including the names of the company directors, maintenance records of any machinery and the ingredients and origin of any food.

> **TIP**
> Inspections can happen at any time but you can expect an inspection as often as once every six months.

At the end of a visit you can expect the following from the officer:

- A summary of what has been found and recorded
- A request for any further information needed from you
- Confirmation of any action you're are required to take as a result of the visit (this can be in the form of a warning letter or notice)
- Confirmation of how long you have to take any required action
- An opportunity for you to make any comments

If you refuse to cooperate, or the officer feels they have been deliberately obstructed from carrying out their duty, you can be prosecuted and fined up to £5,000.

If you disagree with any conclusions the officer comes to you have to right to take the following action:

- Ask to discuss the concerns directly with the officer to reach a compromise
- Ask to speak to the officer's team manager
- Write to the Director of Environmental Services detailing your concerns
- Complain to the local government ombudsman
- Appeal against any notice given to you

Food hygiene

So you've registered your restaurant with the local authority, but what do you need to do in order to prepare for an inspection? The best way to get ready for an inspection is to never actually have to do any extra work for the environmental health officer's visit. In other words, run your restaurant like every day is inspection day.

The most important regulations relating to food preparation are:

- Regulation (EC) No. 852/2004 on the hygiene of foodstuffs
- The Food Hygiene (England) Regulations 2006 (there are equivalent regulations for Scotland, Wales and Northern Ireland).

For more info visit:
www.food.gov.uk/scotland
www.food.gov.uk/wales
www.food.gov.uk/northernireland

These regulations set out the basic requirements for all aspects of a food business including premises, facilities and the hygiene of you and your staff.

You are legally required to put in place 'food safety management procedures' and you must:

- Permanently keep these procedures in place
- Keep up to date documents relating to the procedures
- Review all procedures if you change how you work or the food you produce

 IN MY EXPERIENCE:
Eza Philippe Navaratnasingam, The Lounge

I did a lot of food hygiene courses when I worked in Switzerland and it's far stricter there than in the UK. When I came to England I saw some really shocking kitchens and started to think that's just how people worked over here.'

The regulations are designed to be relatively flexible, meaning smaller restaurants would only need to have simple procedures and documents relating to them, while larger establishments would have more complex procedures.

More detail on the regulations can be obtained from the Food Standards Agency (FSA) but here's a summary of what's required of your restaurant to meet basic standards.

Premises

Every aspect of the restaurant premises must be clean and kept in good condition. The layout and design of the restaurant must:

- Allow for adequate maintenance and cleaning
- Avoid or minimise air-borne contamination
- Provide enough space for you to carry out tasks hygienically
- Protect against dirt build-up
- Allow good hygiene practices
- Provide suitable conditions for handling and storing food

More detail of the legal requirements for restaurant premises can be found in the *Finding premises* and *Decking it out* chapters.

Staff

Every single person working in the food-handling area of the restaurant is required by law to maintain a high level of personal cleanliness. This involves far more than leaving muddy shoes outside the back door or making sure your chef has a clean apron on.

You must also not allow anyone to enter a food-handling area if they:

- Are suffering from, or carrying, a disease likely to be transmitted through food
- Have infected wounds, skin infections or sores
- Have diarrhoea (in this instance staff suffering from the condition must not return to work until 48 hours after the symptoms have disappeared).

Food preparation

All food must be stored and prepared in appropriate conditions, designed to prevent harmful deterioration and protect it from contamination. This includes all stages of preparation from the production of the raw ingredients to when they're served at the customer's table.

There are four Cs to remember when thinking about food hygiene. These are:

- Cross-contamination
- Cleaning
- Chilling
- Cooking

Cross contamination is the most common cause of food poisoning and occurs when harmful bacteria are spread on to food from other food, surfaces, hands or equipment. The kind of harmful bacteria involved in cross contamination usually comes from raw meat, poultry and eggs, so you'll need to take extra care when handling these foods.

Other sources of contamination to be mindful of are staff, pests, equipment and cloths. You should also watch out for both physical and chemical contamination of food, where items such as glass or packaging can fall into food, or substances such as cleaning products or pest controls which could come into contact with it.

Effective cleaning is vital to ensure your restaurant keeps food poisoning at bay. You should devise schedules which include the ongoing cleaning your staff will do throughout the cooking process, at the end of service and the more extensive cleaning done on a less frequent basis.

There's also the issue of making sure your staff are clean from head to toe. This is not an industry where you let a spot of bad personal hygiene slide. You are obligated to address issues of bad cleanliness in any member of staff that comes into contact with food or the food preparation areas.

All 'cold' food must legally be kept at 8°C or lower but it's recommended that you maintain chilled foods at 5°C or lower. Extra care must also be taken when chilling hot food, and when freezing and defrosting.

The following foods must be kept chilled:

- Food with a 'use-by' date
- Food that says 'keep refrigerated' on the label

- Food you have cooked and will not serve immediately
- Ready-to-eat food such as salads and desserts

You should check the temperature of your chilling equipment at least once a day.

Just as much care and attention should be taken when cooking food as preparing it. 'Hot' food must be kept at 63°C or higher. When food is reheated, it must be piping hot all the way through. In Scotland it must be reheated to 82°C before it can be used or served.

There are certain foods that particular attention must be paid to, including eggs, shellfish and rice, as incorrect heating of them can actually foster harmful bacteria.

More detail on the principles and legal requirements of safe food preparation can be found in the FSA guide *Safer Food, Better Business*, which can be downloaded from www.food.gov.uk.

Waste disposal

Your restaurant will generate waste and you need to be aware of your legal responsibilities regarding its disposal. The law requires you to keep all waste tidy and safe. This means ensuring there is a specific area, away from the public where waste can be stored securely, and hygienically, until it's removed.

Under the Environment Protection Act 1990 you must:

- Arrange a trade waste collection agreement with the local authority or an authorised licensed-waste carrier (note: your business rates do not include payment for waste disposal)
- Keep records on the type of waste you give to the collector
- Only put waste out on the street on the day of collection and in proper waste containers so it's contained
- Not, under any circumstances, put commercial waste into litter bins or try to dispose of it via domestic waste collections

Failure to comply with these requirements could result in a fixed penalty notice or a court appearance.

Fire safety

The laws surrounding businesses and their fire safety requirements have undergone significant reform in recent years. The Regulatory Reform (Fire Safety) Order 2005 came into force across England and Wales in October 2006.

The order places emphasis towards risk reduction and fire prevention and means that fire certificates are no longer issued. Instead, you must carry out a fire risk assessment for your premises. The assessment should pay particular attention to those at special risk, such as young people, the disabled and those with special needs. You will also need to produce an emergency plan.

Your local fire authority can give you more details on how to carry out the fire risk assessment and what details you need to include in your emergency plan.

Things to remember:

- Get the right insurance.

- Register with your local authority 28 days before opening.

- Get the right licence under The Licensing Act 2003.

- Make sure your health and safety assessments and procedures are in place and staff are adequately trained.

- Carry out a fire risk assessment.

- Arrange for a collector to dispose of commercial waste.

- Put food safety management procedures in place.

2.5

Finding suppliers

Y ou can hire the best chef in the world but without good ingredients,
the dishes you serve just won't be up to scratch and neither in turn will
your restaurant. It's precisely for this reason that you need a healthy
relationship with the best suppliers you can possibly find. A fine balance must
be struck between the ingredients you can afford and the quality you need to
produce the best food.

   In this chapter you'll find advice on how to find local suppliers and the
advantages this can have for your restaurant. Your relationship with your
supplier is essential to the quality of the food served in your restaurant so
maintaining that relationship is vital. However you must also make sure you're
using that relationship to the best advantage for your business. We also look at
using organic and seasonal ingredients and how these can help keep your menu
fresh and boost your USPs. Check out the advice on sourcing wine suppliers as
well as tips on the quality of other drinks on offer such as water and coffee.

In this chapter we'll cover:

- Ingredients
- Wine
- Other drinks
- Dealing with suppliers

➡ INGREDIENTS

If you were opening a restaurant 20 years ago, the chances of your customers asking where you source your ingredients were pretty slim. Today, some restaurants base their whole USP on where their ingredients are sourced from. Geetie Singh's main USP for The Duke of Cambridge is the ethical and sustainable source of all her ingredients. On a much smaller scale, even chain restaurants such as the Gourmet Burger Kitchen have a range of organic offerings on their menu.

Climate change, BSE, E-coli and foot and mouth disease have all been imprinted on public consciousness and people are now taking the time to ask questions such as: is this free-range, what are the food miles attached to this and are local farmers and producers being supported? Your dream restaurant may not be one that sources all its ingredients from sustainable supplies and only serves free-range and organic meats, but in today's consumer climate, if you haven't yet attached any ethical considerations to your ingredients, it's something you need to do.

Local suppliers

Using local suppliers obviously reduces the amount of food miles your ingredients amass, but there are other benefits to buying close to home. As well as the 'green' advantage, you can strike up a loyal and mutually beneficial relationship with local suppliers who'll often reward the loyalty of the restaurateurs that buy from them.

Another advantage to buying locally is it's much easier to monitor the quality of the ingredients yourself. If you buy directly from farmers, for example, you can see how the animals are reared or how the produce is grown.

> ## ✦ TIP
> The best way to strike up deals with local suppliers is to visit them yourself. You can foster a much closer relationship if you know them personally, and it shows you're taking the time out to understand how they work. Visit the local farms, or go over and have a chat at trade fairs and markets.

Convenience is another crucial advantage of using local suppliers. If your cheese comes from the other side of the country, what happens when you unexpectedly run out? Local suppliers are far more willing to accommodate extra orders, not to mention more quickly!

Seasonal and sustainable ingredients

Restricting your ingredients to those that are currently in season and sustainable obviously has its limitations but there are plenty of benefits too. Firstly, it forces you to keep your menu up-to-date and varied, as you'll have to make alterations to it throughout the year.

Secondly, only buying seasonal or sustainable foods will reduce the carbon footprint of your restaurant, as you won't be shipping in food from the other side of the world to meet your demands. The issue of importing out of season foods is a controversial topic at the moment, and celebrity chef Gordon Ramsay recently sparked debate when he suggested restaurants should be fined for doing it.

Lastly, a massive advantage of only using seasonal food is quality. If you buy fresh produce currently in season it's not only healthier but also tastes better, which is reason enough for the best chefs and the most discerning customers.

 IN MY EXPERIENCE:
Geetie Singh, The Duke of Cambridge

'If I hadn't worked in a wholefood shop before starting the restaurant it would have been a very difficult to find the right suppliers. My chef would say to me: "Where do I get bulk organic tinned tomatoes?", and I could say "there are none" because I knew that from working in the wholefood shop.'

Organic

It's still a hotly debated issue – whether or not organic food is actually better for you and the earth or just has a superior taste. Either way, organic food is big business and increasing numbers of people go out of their way to find all-natural produce. Certain organic foods such as fresh fruit and vegetables are more popular than others, so if a completely organic menu isn't possible, you may want

to pepper it with specific items. For more info on organic food visit
www.soilassociation.org.

Overseas ingredients

You'll need a very specific type of menu to avoid buying any ingredients from
abroad. Modern cooking requires ingredients from all over the world which
can be expensive as well as environmentally questionable. Think carefully about
where you source your produce from, and try to plan in advance to avoid
unnecessary repeat orders. Be economical too. The internet allows you to shop
all over the world from the confines of your restaurant so use it to your advantage.

FROM THE EXPERTS:
Iqbal Wahhab, The Cinnamon Club and Roast

'All Roast's fruit and vegetables come from Borough Market. We primarily use the
meat suppliers from the market too, but the fish suppliers are only here
three days a week so we can't always use them. The concept behind Roast is
about celebrating British Food and what better way to do that than to use all this
fantastic British produce that we have right here in the market?'

Some handy contact details for finding suppliers:

www.localfoodworks.org
www.bigbarn.co.uk
www.thefoody.com
www.britishcompanies.co.uk/food.htm
www.greenchoices.org
www.halalfoodauthority.co.uk

Use the internet as a research tool for any specific suppliers you want
in your area. Most suppliers will have a web presence so take some time
out to see what the options are in your area.

➡ WINE

Depending on what kind of restaurant you're running, your range and display of drinks will have varied significance to the business. Some restaurants such as many Indian restaurants do not serve alcohol at all, negating the need for a licence. Instead they allow customers to bring their own beer and wine. However, the vast majority of restaurants are licensed to serve alcohol. For more information on obtaining a licence, see the *Getting legal* chapter.

Your choice of wine will say a lot about your restaurant. Fine dining establishments will have a list practically as long as novel, where as more casual places tend to stick to a selection of about 6–10 different reds and whites, a couple of rosés and perhaps a bottle or two of sparkling wine or Champagne.

The important thing is to stick to what suits your restaurant. If your average main costs £12, customers aren't likely to spend £60 on a bottle of wine. Likewise be careful about having too many lower-end wines on the menu that are readily available in off-licences and the supermarket. There's an accepted mark up on wine served in restaurants, but customers won't knowingly pay £17 for a bottle they regularly buy for £8 to drink at home.

When choosing house wines make sure they're a decent standard. Your customers won't expect them to be the best on the menu, but they'll want something better than just palatable. Avoid choosing house wines that are too heavy or oaky. There's plenty of room for distinctive flavours further down your wine list.

FROM THE EXPERTS:
Iqbal Wahhab, The Cinnamon Club and Roast

'I have a theory that nobody spends less on a bottle of wine than their main course. If a customer orders a £31 main, they'll spend £45–£50 on a bottle of wine.'

Wine suppliers

In order to get a good deal and be certain what you're getting is quality wine, you need to either know your stuff when it comes to tasting, or get someone on board who does. Send yourself on a couple of tasting courses so you get to know the basic principles. Arm yourself with knowledge so that when you come to deal with suppliers you'll know exactly want you want and need for the restaurant.

Here's a few tips for dealing with wine suppliers:

- Get some price lists before you arrange a sales meeting. It's easy to get sucked in by a sales pitch, taste wines you love and order a whole batch before you realise what you're being sold is actually out of your budget.
- Check what kind of quantities you can order in. Is it flexible or do you need to buy a minimum number of cases? You may not have enough storage space for the minimum order requirements of some suppliers.
- Arrange tasting sessions at the restaurant, supplier's premises or even trade shows where you can sample wines from plenty of different sources.
- Ask what the supplier can provide you with other than wine. Will they train your staff, compile your drinks menus, provide you with glasses? It's surprising what you can get thrown in if you just negotiate a bit.
- If possible, try to negotiate as flexible a contract as possible. You don't want to be tied in to buying 30 bottles a month of a particular wine that just isn't selling in your restaurant.
- Finally, don't feel the need to buy all your wine from one supplier. A varied list will not only make your wine list unique, but allow you to shop around for the best deals on different varieties of wine.

IN MY EXPERIENCE:

Lisa Tse, Sweet Mandarin

'We were approached by a wine supplier while we were building the restaurant. A guy just turned up on the doorstep and asked us to try some wines. We did, and we liked them so we asked what he could do for us. He did our menus, gave us some samples and a price list. We've been with the same wine merchant ever since.'

➡ DRINKS

Coffee

Despite the rise in American-style coffee bar chains over the last decade many of your customers will still be coffee purists. It's unlikely your diners will want to finish their meal with a jumbo-size mocha latte, so unless your restaurant is US-themed stick to good quality European-style coffee.

As well as arming your restaurant with a decent espresso machine and/or filter coffee maker, choose a good-quality bean. If you're planning to use plenty of organic or FairTrade ingredients on your menu, stay consistent and apply this to your choice of coffee.

> ## ⚓ TIP
> Another point to remember, and one which many restaurants and cafés seem to be confused about, is the difference between filter coffee and an Americano. A filter coffee involves all the water used being passed through the coffee grounds. An Americano, on the other hand, is an espresso topped up with hot water. Don't confuse the two, and make sure they're identified correctly on your menu.

Water

The water served in restaurants has proved a controversial issue in recent years. Many restaurants have come under for fire for pushing sales of bottled water as opposed to providing tap water to customers for free. While there is no legal requirement to provide free tap water, you may find your diners don't take kindly to having to pay, and probably won't grace you with their custom again if you try and charge for it.

Likewise, don't kick up a fuss when a customer asks for tap water instead of bottled water. It's bad customer service and you'll lose more from upsetting your diners than any mark up you would have gained on selling a bottle of Evian.

The Italian-style restaurant chain Strada serves tap water in decorative branded glass bottles, making the customer feel they're getting a little more than just tap water when they're not.

Some restaurants serve their customers tap water as a matter of routine as soon as they're seated. Of course it's up to you whether or not you wish to do this. On the plus side it may earn you brownie points for service, but on the other hand it may discourage customers from ordering things with a mark up such as bottled water or soft drinks. It's unlikely to deter customers from ordering a bottle of wine however.

➡ DEALING WITH SUPPLIERS

Your menu may already be printed before you make arrangements with suppliers. However, you may find that you tailor it according to the kind of supplier network you have available to you. If your restaurant has a rural location for example, you may want to advertise the fact that your meat comes from a particular local farm, or your cheese comes from a nearby dairy.

Your food purchasing decisions can make or break your restaurant so consider your supplier network carefully, keep it under constant review and always go for quality over convenience.

IN MY EXPERIENCE:

Lisa Tse, Sweet Mandarin

'Finding suppliers wasn't really that hard for us because we had a lot of contacts in the Chinese cash and carry industry. But knowing how much of everything you need to buy can be really difficult at first. When you've just opened a restaurant there's often a tendency to overbuy before you realise exactly how much you need.'

Before deciding on your suppliers and the source of your ingredients you need to establish who is responsible for doing the buying. It may be yourself, your head chef or a manager. Whoever the responsibility lies with, this person needs to be aware of the portions needed for each dish, the level of quality expected, how the ingredients will be used and what kind of price limits must be stuck to.

Choosing suppliers

Do your research carefully and compare as many options as possible before agreeing to any provision of service. If possible visit the premises of the companies and individuals you're buying from. If not, then make sure you've tasted and tested everything you plan to order.

> **TIP**
>
> Where possible buy directly from the growers, producers and
> manufacturers. That's were you'll get the most for your money. When you buy
> from wholesalers remember there's already been at least one mark up by the time
> it gets to you.

Tips for choosing suppliers:

- Be as detailed and as thorough as possible with your lists. Organise it
  into sections – wine, cheese, meat, dried or tinned goods etc. If you can
  be as specific as possible before you start choosing suppliers you'll know
  exactly what you need and won't run the risk of being sold unnecessary
  produce.
- Get recommendations. Ask other restaurateurs who they use, who they've had
  trouble with in the past and who they'd recommend.
- Have at least two suppliers available for every ingredient you need. You may
  have one that you prefer or use nearly all the time, but it's good to have a
  back-up.
- Visit trade shows and go to food tastings. Visit local farmers' markets and
  build up your contact base.
- Negotiate terms and conditions. Check delivery terms. Can they supply you at
  short notice if you have a sudden busy period? Can they offer you a discount
  for long-term/ repeat orders? Can you agree fixed prices for a certain period
  of time?

Maintaining the relationship

Once you've established a network of suppliers you're happy with and can rely on,
it's important you maintain a good working relationship with them. It's not just
about paying your bills on time.

- Try to deal with the same sales representative or agent whenever you order.
  Building a relationship with one person is more likely to inspire trust and the
  odd favour when you need it.

- Keep a check on prices and review your bills against what other suppliers are offering. Even if you don't want to change suppliers you may be able to negotiate more competitive prices.
- Check the quality of all food when it arrives at the restaurant. If something's wrong with it, politely but firmly ask for replacements. Don't let quality slide. Your suppliers need to keep up their end of the bargain.

IN MY EXPERIENCE:

Eza Philippe Navaratnasingam, The Lounge

I buy all the ingredients myself as and when they're needed. I visit the fruit and veg markets as necessary, the butchers twice a week and the cash and carry once a week. I do it because I like to check all my ingredients before I buy them. I even bought a mincer so I could mince my own steak here at the restaurant. It's a lot of work but for me it's worth it because I know exactly what goes into the food.'

Building good credit

The relationship between you and your suppliers is an important one. Regardless of whether they're a cash and carry, a farmer, a grower or a wholesaler, you have the right to expect a quality product, delivered on time for a reasonable price. In return, your supplier will expect to be paid on time, and in a manner that suits them.

IN MY EXPERIENCE:

Shevonne Bennett, Brown Sugar

'If you're starting on limited funds don't mess around with suppliers. Be honest with them and they'll be reasonable with you. Small businesses are a long-term investment for them so they want you to do well.'

It's best to lay your cards on the table when agreeing to payment terms with suppliers. Agree dates and stick to them, but ask for payment terms that are reasonable and achievable for you to manage.

Start missing payment dates and your suppliers will soon get tired and may drop you from their client base. Once you get into a spiral of debt and bad credit

it can be hard to climb out of it. You'll soon find that the network of decent
suppliers available to you is smaller than originally imagined and the last thing
you want to do is sacrifice the quality of your ingredients because of a couple of
late cheques.

Things to remember:

● Keep a healthy balance between affordable
  ingredients and noticeable quality.

● If possible, meet your suppliers in person before you
  start ordering from them.

● Taste all the wines you put on your menu, and make
  sure there's enough of a range to suit all tastes.

● Don't tag a charge for tap water on to the bill. It won't
  go down well with customers.

● Don't feel obliged to order everything from the same
  few suppliers. Constantly reassess to check if you're
  getting the best deal.

Recruiting staff

The people you employ to help run your restaurant will have just as much influence over its success as the food you serve, so it's crucial that you get the right team on board. Recruitment is a tricky area, and one that ends up being extremely costly if you make bad decisions.

Like your business plan you have to plan carefully and decide what roles you need filled, be that an experienced head chef or a kitchen porter you will need to train up, as well as the number of staff your restaurant will need to be a success. This chapter will guide you from defining the kind of team you need, through the recruitment process, to the paperwork you will need to file once you hire someone. It also contains advice on training your staff to ensure your restaurant reaches its full potential.

In this chapter we'll cover:

- What your staffing needs are
- Job roles
- Recruitment
- Interviewing
- Training

➡ WHAT ARE YOUR STAFFING NEEDS?

Your business plan should have included an idea of how many members of staff you'll need to run your restaurant smoothly, but also will have taken into account what you can afford. Ask yourself the following questions:

- Will you be recruiting a head chef, or will you be taking on the cooking duties yourself?
- How many people will you need in the kitchen, and what roles will they take on? Will you need a sous chef, a commis chef and a kitchen porter?
- How many waiting staff will you need?
- Will you employ a dedicated cleaner or will this fall under the remit of other staff?
- How many days/hours will your staff work? Which staff will you need to double up on to make sure you always have the right number of employees working on any given day?
- Which members of staff will work part-time and who will you need to employ on a full-time basis?

Take a look at our sample staff rota at the back of this book for a rough guide to working this out.

Once you've established exactly how many members of staff your restaurant needs you will have to make a decision on what you can afford to pay them. You'll need to strike a fine balance between being practical and not stretching your budget too far, but also being realistic about what you need to pay to attract the right kind of talent.

The restaurant industry is booming and good staff are hard to come by. You may find that you need to budget more than you'd intended to find friendly and efficient staff the create the restaurant atmosphere you're trying to achieve.

➡ DISTINGUISHING JOB ROLES

Head chef

This is the most important role in the kitchen and unless you're taking on this role yourself, choosing your head chef will be your most important recruitment decision. You'll want someone with passion and flair but also someone who is dedicated, and above all, reliable.

IN MY EXPERIENCE:
Geetie Singh, The Duke of Cambridge

'Head chefs are difficult. That's the hardest and most key person to find. Sometimes I dream up a new concept and then wonder how I'd find a head chef to suit it. The fact is it's just hard and I can't really offer any help for that. We were really lucky and found a wonderful chef who really knew what she was doing. She came highly recommended from a prestigious place. After Caroline, we just trained and promoted from within, and I've only out twice since then.'

What you require from your head chef will vary depending on what size and type of establishment you're running, but may include all or some of the following:

- Creating dishes and preparing meals
- Planning menus
- Managing the kitchen and restaurant staff
- Ordering supplies
- Training junior kitchen staff
- Putting in an appearance with customers as the face of the restaurant

Chefs have a bit of a reputation for being somewhat headstrong and unruly. However, combined with the right personality traits this can be exactly what you need for a successful restaurant.

You'll want to find someone with great menu ideas who'll adapt and respond to your vision for the restaurant. However, finding someone exceptionally talented for your kitchen may at times mean your own ideas are challenged. This can result in conflict, but can also keep you on your toes and keep your ideas fresh, so don't shy away from someone just because you think they'll challenge you.

IN MY EXPERIENCE:
Shevonne Bennett, Brown Sugar

'Finding the right staff was so hard. I went through a series of chefs that didn't work out, and ended up having to do the cooking myself for the first six months. I think the recruitment process was something I overlooked initially because the whole start-up process happened so fast.'

Sous chef

Depending on how big a restaurant you plan on running you may not have anyone cooking other than your head chef. However, if you have a team of chefs in the kitchen your sous chef will be second in command, do a lot of the cooking and be in charge when the head chef isn't in the kitchen.

Commis chef

This is the first rung on the chef ladder for those that have just recently trained in the catering profession. The commis chef will do a lot of the preparation work such as chopping ingredients or plating garnishes. Again, depending on the size of kitchen you have, you may not have a need for a commis chef early on.

Kitchen porter

This person is generally responsible for washing-up, keeping the kitchen clean and tidy and perhaps some basic food preparation depending on what the chefs require.

Maitre d'

This person runs front of house operations in the restaurant. If you start off small, you may take on this role yourself. The maitre d' is in charge of managing the waiting staff on duty, seating diners and, in less favourable circumstances, dealing with complaints. This person needs to be friendly and personable as they'll have the job of greeting diners.

➡ WRITING RECRUITMENT ADS AND SHORTLISTING

Before drawing up a recruitment advertisement you need to have worked out the duties and level of responsibility included in the role. You need to define the vacant position accurately and be clear about exactly what type of person you want for the role.

IN MY EXPERIENCE:

Geetie Singh, The Duke of Cambridge

'When recruiting I used a lot of the connections I'd already built up from the people I'd worked with before. We also advertised in the Evening Standard. That stuff was quite straightforward for me because I'd been doing it for so long.'

The recruitment ad should be clear and brief. You should list the job requirements, criteria for applicants, salary and contract length. When listing skills requirements be sure to include only those that are strictly necessary for the role. You may want your kitchen porter to have had experience in a Michelin-starred restaurant, but think about whether it's really necessary find someone that experienced for a menial role. Likewise, for your head chef you may want to state what level of experience is required. For example, experience of working in large kitchen managing several other chefs.

Describe your restaurant, or what you intend it to be like, and give its location. You don't want to be wasting time answering queries from potential applicants that don't live close enough, or aren't willing to move to the local area. Also remember to clearly state the application process. How should people apply? By phone, in writing, or via email?

Where you advertise will depend on the role and also the type of establishment you're running. For more senior positions such as the head chef, try catering industry magazines or websites such as www.caterer.com or *The Hotelkeeper*.

A good place to meet potential employees is industry networking events. At these types of events you'll be able to meet people and gather first impressions without the formal process of interviewing.

For lower level roles within the restaurant there are the more traditional recruitment routes such as local papers, the job centre, recruitment agencies and online.

Your chance to apply discretion about the people you hire will come during the shortlisting process. Remember, that at this stage it's your opportunity to sell your restaurant as best you can to attract the highest calibre of talent. You can't run your restaurant without good staff so it's crucial you get them interested in your establishment.

Once you've received applications for a role, remember that all the information you receive is confidential. When faced with an overwhelming number of applications, try to avoid random screening methods such as disregarding everyone with a particular postcode. You may find you've ruled out the ideal employee this way.

Try using checklists of essential criteria relating the job specifications you drew up when writing the ad or defining the job role. You must screen all applications using this criteria and nothing else – be aware of any personal prejudices you may have fallen back on.

Get the recruitment process right and you greatly reduce the risk of attracting the wrong kind of people in the first place. Mess it up and you won't even find a suitable candidate to pick from a pile of a hundred CVs, let alone be able to spot them at interview stage.

Invest your time during the recruitment stage as it can be an extremely expensive process. You don't want to eat away at your start-up funds by spending money on recruitment ads that aren't attracting the kind of staff you want and need for your restaurant. If you don't want to spend any cash on recruitment there's always the traditional note in the window.

➡ INTERVIEWING

Successful interviewing requires certain skills. If you've never employed people before you may find some training helpful. For more information on training contact the Chartered Institute of Personnel and Development at www.cipd.co.uk. There are various courses available to teach you effective interviewing techniques, but if you can't spare the time or finances for these, we'll cover the basics here.

Interviews must be planned extremely carefully. You only have a short window of time to elicit all the information you need for a potential recruit. Not only do you have to ascertain their relevant levels of experience, you also need to gauge accurate impressions about whether they fit in with the kind of atmosphere you're trying to achieve.

IN MY EXPERIENCE:
Geetie Singh, The Duke of Cambridge

'We held interviews from our freezing windowless office above the pub that our landlord had let us use, wearing woolly hats and gloves.'

After coming up with a shortlist for interview, you should contact prospective interviewees and give them clear instructions on where you're located, how to get there, what they should bring with them, who they should ask for and how long the process is likely to last. Set aside some dedicated time to do the interviews – make sure there are no unnecessary interruptions like ringing phones. If you've already found your restaurant premises then it's a good idea to conduct the interview there.

Remember, the interview stage is just as much about you selling yourself and the restaurant to them as the other way around. The best candidates are always going to be in high demand so you'll need to impress them too if you want to attract them to your restaurant.

Before the interviews make sure you have a series of appropriate questions prepared, bearing in mind what you need to find out about the candidates. This will include general questions regarding their personality, as well as questions that probe more deeply into how well suited they are to the job. Make sure you stick to these basic questions when interviewing all the candidates. Of course further questions will arise depending on the candidates you're speaking to, but you need to make sure you've covered the same basic format with everyone.

There are also some legal implications to be aware of during the interview stage. It's natural to want to find out as much about the candidate as possible but there are certain questions that you simply must NOT ask, or you could leave yourself vulnerable to discrimination claims. These include:

- Race – avoid questions about ethnic background or country of origin. In the restaurant trade you may find this is something that naturally comes up when talking about different kinds of food. However, there'll be time for that if you decided to take the candidate on. Avoid the subject during interview.
- Gender – there are the obvious sexist comments to avoid, but something you may slip up on is asking about families. Avoid asking about a candidate's future plans to have children etc.
- Disability – obviously there are certain disabilities that would prevent certain restaurant roles. However, if it only involves certain adjustments to enable a disabled person to do the job you have to consider them as equally as all other candidates.

As a new restaurateur, at this stage, it's likely you'll be the sole interviewer, or perhaps it'll be you and a partner. At a later point you may be able to share or delegate this responsibility on to your manager or head chef. The advantage of this is you can discuss your opinions of each candidate.

Once you've interviewed all the candidates it's time to make a decision. Try and let your notes and any scoring system you devised guide you as much as possible.

However, a restaurant is a people business and you'll need the right people to make it work, so personality is inevitably going to sway you. That's fine, as long as it's not at the expense of other qualities such as reliability and efficiency.

Once you've made an offer, the next step is to check references. How you do this is up to you, but your options are through written correspondence, by telephone or in person. Once you've checked the candidates' references you can confirm their start date and begin the administrative process of taking on an employee.

➡ THE PAPERWORK

Becoming an employer for the first time can seem a little daunting. There's a whole raft of administrative duties you'll now be responsible for, and neglecting them is not an option.

Your first point of call should be to contact HMRC on 0845 60 70 143 and request a New Employer Starter Pack. It contains everything you need to set yourself up to recruit staff.

Nearly everyone that will work in your restaurant will count as an employee, which means you need to be aware of your obligations for tax and National Insurance contributions. You must keep detailed records of every single member of staff right from the very beginning. All of the following types of staff count as employees in the eyes of the taxman:

- Directors
- Full and part-time workers
- Temporary or casual workers

Even if a worker claims to be self-employed and will pay their own tax and National Insurance, as an employer it is your responsibility to confirm that. HMRC will offer you guidance on how to do this in the Starter Pack.

Of course, making sure your employees' tax is in order isn't the only obligation you have. Make sure you also know your legal responsibilities regarding:

- Statutory sick and maternity pay
- Working time and pay regulations
- National Minimum Wage
- Redundancy pay

- Employing foreign nationals
- Part-time workers' regulations

Training

Certain members of staff you hire will undoubtedly have had the right kind of training in catering and food hygiene. If your head chef isn't skilled in the principles of good kitchen practice then you should seriously be re-evaluating your recruitment process. However, there are other members of your staff that may need to be trained up to comply with the minimum legal standards.

We've covered the specific legal acts businesses that prepare food are bound by in more detail in the *Getting Legal* chapter, but one important thing to remember is all the staff in your restaurant that handle food must have the appropriate training.

Once your staff are all up to speed on food preparation requirements you'll want to educate them in the ways of how you run your particular establishment. Much of this will need to be done before you open. Learning on the job is all well and good but come opening night, you'll need waiters and kitchen staff that are on the ball and working together smoothly.

Before you open, why not have friends and family round so that your new staff have a chance to put all their skills into action before the paying customers arrive. That way you'll be able to identify any areas where more training is required, and whether you're in a position to provide the training yourself or assess whether outside help is needed.

IN MY EXPERIENCE:

Ian Pengelley, Gilgamesh

'I do a lot of training with my staff. If your managers can't train the waiters then you have to do it yourself. They're ambassadors for the food and the restaurant. In turn, if the customers enjoy the food it makes the waiters proud. The whole process is all about teamwork and it starts at the front door right through to the kitchen.'

Things to remember:

- Try to keep a flexible approach to staffing numbers when you first start. You may need to keep some staff on stand-by while you get a feel for the average number of diners you'll have.

- Work out exactly what you require in each role before you start recruiting for the job.

- As well as agencies and job adverts, put an ad in your window for casual staff such as cleaners or waiters.

- Be careful not to fall into any interview traps regarding questions about personal or family life. It could land you in hot water and contravene employment law.

Hestons wanted.

The importance of working with commercial equipment

1. Domestic Vs commercial equipment

As your kitchen is the pulse of your business, it is crucial to understand the difference between domestic equipment and commercial appliances. At first glance you may regard home equipment as a low cost alternative however, domestic equipment is not designed to endure large workloads. Commercial equipment can withstand the heat and humidity that builds-up throughout the day and is built with additional safety features including heavy-duty power cords and overload switches. Commercial equipment is generally easier to operate and maintain and stainless steel is easy to clean, hygienic and ensures your appliances last longer.

2. Cutting costs can be a risky business

When you choose equipment that cannot match the needs of your busy kitchen team, you not only risk your food quality, but additional dangers include cross-contamination and general safety. Commercial refrigeration is the perfect example of the importance of investing in quality equipment. Commercial fridges are designed with special installation features, helping them withstand extreme temperatures and reducing the likeliness of breakdown. Many models come equipped with drip-trays, which reduce the risk of cross-contamination and keep food fresh, and those with automatic defrost and electronic thermostats can improve energy efficiency and durability.

3. Making your equipment work with you

Investing in quality equipment does not have to be an expensive business – you just have to be fully aware of your objectives and find a professional supplier you can trust. Firstly, consider your menus and chef's capabilities and decide what equipment is necessary; overloading your kitchen with unnecessary appliances is simply a waste of your resources. Taking care of your equipment can also help maintain long life and robustness. And most importantly, working with a professional company like Chiller Box, who will carefully consider your operational requirements and provide unbiased advice on a full range of products, will ensure you receive the best for your new business.

The opening

N ow that you've worked so hard to get your restaurant ready for launch, there's the challenge of actually running it to look forward to. Before you can do that however, you need to get the customers through the door. You will need to decide what kind of advertising will work best for you, be that press releases, print ads or online advertising, and whether you want to hire a professional PR firm to organise this campaign for you.

In this chapter we'll take you through the process of getting ready for launch, achieving the right level of publicity and making sure diners are queuing up on opening night.

In this chapter we'll cover:

- PR
- Advertising
- First impressions
- Soft openings
- Launch parties

➡ ADVERTISING AND PR

You may feel that you don't need to formally advertise your restaurant. Free PR and promotions can often be more effective depending on what kind of establishment you're running. However, if you do decide to take out paid-for ads, you need a clear understanding of how the industry works. With either option you need to plan your strategy carefully.

Hiring a PR company

There's no average price for taking on a PR company. It's entirely dependent on the level of service you want and the reputation of the company you choose. However, for more guidance on what it's likely to cost to promote your restaurant contact the Public Relations Consultants Association. You can fill out an online application detailing your requirements and they'll send you a list of recommended companies who can then come up with a tailored plan and quotation for you. Visit www.prca.org.uk for more details.

PR

Effective PR can be invaluable in terms of the kind of coverage you can get for your restaurant, both in its early stages and throughout its existence. There's more detail on how to get continued exposure in the media in the *Ongoing Marketing* chapter, but it is something you should think hard about before opening night.

 IN MY EXPERIENCE:
Ian Pengelley, Gilgamesh

'You really have to get the right PR people in if you want to get the right message across. Get the press on side. I was lucky because when *Pengelley's* shut there was a lot of press surrounding it, so when I came back on the scene I still had this press connection with Ramsay. All the press were writing about Gilgamesh opening and wondering if it was going to be another disaster – the next car crash restaurant in London! But I worked incredibly hard with the critics to make sure I didn't make mistakes. Although we did have some initial bad reviews regarding the service, we'd made sure all the dishes were perfected before we opened and that got us good reviews.'

As a rule, the press like new things so if you're clever about it, you can make news out of the opening of your restaurant. One of the ways to do that is to send out a press release. At first glance, most press releases look simple but even the biggest companies agonise over them. There's a skill to writing a press release and if you haven't written one before you should take some advice before you start. You may want to hire a PR company to take care of everything from writing press releases to organising your launch party. However, if this is out of your budget, here are some useful tips for writing a press release:

- Make sure the wording is correct, the message is clear and direct and the correct information is provided so that a journalist will be able to use it even if they do not contact a member of your company or public relations team.
- Your release should convey a sense of importance but not seem over-hyped. You want to provide information about your firm in a newsy format, not a marketing letter. Besides, if your announcement is worth sending a release out about, it can probably stand on its own without marketing hype.
- All press releases should answer the journalist's five basic questions of: Who, What, Where, Why and How. This will require you to put yourself in the shoes of a journalist and chances are, answering those questions will give you a clearer idea of what you want to write.
- A punchy headline should be included that matches the release's first sentence, or lead, as those in the trade call them. The headline should be factual. It shouldn't try to make a joke or be smart.
- The first sentence should be direct, relate what is going on, convey a level of importance of the news and start off with the name of your restaurant.
- Include a quote from you or your head chef. It can personalise it and give the journalist an idea of who to speak to. Most journalists will seek their own quotes by following up releases with interviews, but having a quote gives journalists the option to use it.
- Contact details for journalists who want to find out more can either go at the top of the release or the bottom.

One thing to remember is journalists get inundated with hundreds of releases and in truth, most end up in the bin because they aren't directed to a person. Avoid sending your press release cold. Phone up first and find out who the best person to send it to is and follow up a day or two later to pursue the story.

IN MY EXPERIENCE:

Geetie Singh, The Duke of Cambridge

'I do everything I can in terms of PR. You need to in the restaurant industry because it's all about word of mouth. When we launched we sent out press releases informing people that we were the first organic gastropub and it just rollercoastered from there. We didn't have to do an awful lot more after that but I would still send out the odd press release for things like when we launched our fish policy which was approved by the Marine Conservation Society. We did a big press launch and invited journalists to do a quiz night with a fish and chip supper for free.'

Print ads

The most common forms of print advertising that small businesses use are:

- Local/regional/national newspapers
- Trade journals
- Trade directories
- Telephone directories eg Yellow Pages
- Miscellaneous items such as calendars, local tourist information

Newspapers and magazines should provide an audited readership profile, which can be matched to the customer profile to identify if they'll attract the right kind of customers to your restaurant. They should be able to provide you with information on their circulation, which is the amount of copies that go out. Avoid advertising in publications without this kind of audited data.

TIP

While it's important to do your research on the circulation of whoever you advertise with, bear in mind that free newspapers and magazines may have a readership lower than the official circulation. In contrast, those with a cover price usually have a readership larger than circulation.

In terms of size, generally, the bigger the better if budget permits, although allowing editorial onto the page either at the bottom or the left-hand side can actually help. You should also bear in mind that as print ads are repeated the impact lessens. It can, therefore, be better to spend the budget on a few high impact ads than a lot of small ones. But test the waters slowly. Don't blow your whole marketing budget on a massive ad campaign in the local newspaper only to find print ads aren't the right medium for you.

Publishers will quote you different rates for different positions and sizes. Prime spots such as near the front or in the news sections, right hand pages, or tops of pages cost about 20% more but as a rule are worth the extra investment because they're viewed by the most readers. If you're going to splash out on an advert to let people know you're open for business you could use the opportunity to run a special offer. Something encouraging the first customers to walk through the door – a free glass of wine on opening night perhaps.

Sample prices

A quarter-page ad in a local paper can cost upwards of £250 depending on its circulation. A full-page ad in a national paper such as *The Daily Mail* can cost in the region of £30,000

There's more on the value and use of special offers in the *Ongoing Marketing* chapter.

IN MY EXPERIENCE:
Lisa Tse, Sweet Mandarin

'We did a lot of PR when we first opened. We launched a competition to name the restaurant before it even opened. We asked everyone in Manchester to come up with a good name and the winner would get £2,000. We also did something called the Asia Babe competition where we went round to student nights and clubs and invited people to enter a competition to come and work for us.'

Online advertising

Print advertising isn't necessarily the most effective medium anymore. Another way of increasing awareness of your restaurant presence is pay-per-click (PPC) advertising online. Unlike with print or broadcast advertising, with PPC you are only charged when someone actually clicks on your ad. The big player for this type of advertising is Google's AdWords where companies bid for certain keywords relating to their business. Search terms such as Italian restaurant are likely to have an extremely high price, but you may find you can rank quite well for a lot less for a term such as 'Italian restaurant in Isleworth'. Depending on how much you bid, your ad will come up with varying prominence on the listing pages when someone does a search using those keywords.

Advertising isn't the only way to promote your restaurant online however. There are plenty of sites such as Toptable.co.uk and Trustedplaces.com which can bring in customers if used correctly. Check out the *Ongoing Marketing* chapter for more details on getting your restaurant online.

➡ SOFT OPENINGS AND LAUNCH PARTIES

First impressions

A lot of restaurants get it spectacularly wrong during their first few weeks of being open and unfortunately, it's enough to do the damage when it comes to word-of-mouth. Competition in the restaurant trade is stiffer than ever so you can't afford to leave your new customers disappointed. With so many outlets to choose from, what possible reason do they have to come back to a restaurant that didn't serve great food with excellent service?

Unless you've got plans to rename and refurbish your restaurant every couple of months, it's important to remember you only have one chance at a first impression. If you've marketed your launch successfully, you could well have food critics and journalists, local or national, there on opening night. You need to make sure front of house is running smoothly, even if things are a bit chaotic behind the scenes.

> ## ✦ TIP
> Don't launch before you're ready. It can be tempting if you're running behind schedule to just open the doors and hope for the best. However, customers don't want to see a wall that's in need of one more layer of paint, or be waiting 20 minutes for their drinks because you haven't found enough waiting staff yet.

While it's inevitable that many of your staff will learn a lot on the job, they need to be trained enough to provide a comfortable and pleasant dining experience for your first customers. More than any, these are the diners you need to send home satisfied.

Soft launch

A good method for testing the waters, training your staff and ironing out any obvious kinks in your operation before properly launching is to have a soft launch. This is where you can open a few nights a week, or even just for an hour or two during the evening and let passing customers come in and try a meal, perhaps for a discounted rate. The point of this is you won't have advertised the restaurant as open yet, so shouldn't be inundated with customers.

> **IN MY EXPERIENCE:**
> ## Shevonne Bennett, Brown Sugar
>
> 'Before launching I started an e-newsletter about the restaurant and emailed it to all my blue-chip company contacts that I'd built up while working in HR. We then did a mini launch with £10 a head offers.'

Operating at a discounted rate while you break the restaurant in will also mean you can make a few mistakes and learn from them without too much complaining from your customers. Charging full price on your opening night could end up being disastrous in terms of word-of-mouth if customers feel they've spent a lot of money on a restaurant that isn't operating to a good enough standard yet.

> **TIP**
> Use this opportunity to get your customers to fill in a questionnaire on the food, service, price and restaurant atmosphere. Ask them to rate each of these factors from 1 to 5. We've mocked up an example at the back of the book.

Launch party

We've already mentioned the option of hiring a PR company to get you some coverage for opening day or organise a launch party for you. PR companies are easy enough to find online, but if you decide to hire one, make sure you shop around for the best deal and if possible go with a recommendation. One place to try and get advice is from other entrepreneurs. If you don't have the time to go to networking events try the Startups.co.uk forum and ask other start-up business owners who they employed. They may be able to recommend a great PR company, or even warn you off the ones they had trouble with.

You don't have to have a launch party of course, and you shouldn't feel pressured into believing you need one to make an impact in the community. But if you do, make sure you have plenty of sample food on offer from your actual menu. Give people an idea of the kind of food they're likely to expect when the restaurant properly opens for business and if they like it, they'll spread the word.

✦ TIP

Don't go overboard budget-wise when it comes to launch parties. View them as a way to celebrate and reward all the hard work you've gone through in getting to this stage, and a way of generating enough publicity to attract your first customers come opening day.

Things to remember:

- Don't pay for advertising where free PR can be more effective.

- Test out the menu and restaurant on family and friends first.

- Next, bring in a few customers at a discounted rate for a soft launch.

- If you decide to have a launch party, make sure it gets you the desired publicity, but remember to have fun – after all, it's your special night.

3

You're open

Surviving the first six months

The launch party is over. You've had the first few customers through the door. You've hired your staff. The food is making its way out of the kitchen and reaching the diners. But the battle's far from won. Now comes the mammoth task of actually making what you've been planning and preparing for all these months start working.

After that initial excitement of 'The Opening' is over you need to be prepared for an inevitably slow beginning. But this can be a great opportunity to hone your operation and make sure everything is running perfectly. It can also be a good time to reassess your USPs, update your menu and try out different opening times to see what works best for you. This is the time when you learn to deal with complaints and what to do if a restaurant critic walks through the door. The first few months are a matter of survival.

In this chapter we'll cover:

- Preparing for a slow start
- Difficult customers
- The critics
- Assessing your idea
- Updating your menu
- Contingency budgets
- Pricing
- Seasonal variations
- Opening hours

➡ BUILDING UP CUSTOMERS

Preparing for a slow start

Depending on how successful your marketing was, or how many passing customers are instantly attracted to your menu, you should prepare for your first few weeks to be fairly slow. This is not necessarily a bad thing, as it can give you a chance to hone your operation. A slower start allows you to perfect things, test your ideas and assess what works.

IN MY EXPERIENCE:

Lisa Tse, Sweet Mandarin

'You expect people to just walk through the door and it just isn't the case. When we first opened it was quite busy because people wanted to try us out, but there are times when day-to-day tasks can be quite intense. You have to learn to separate your day-to-day management from actually running the business.'

As your reputation in the area builds, so too should your customer base, and with a gradual build up in the number of diners you should have the whole restaurant running with as few flaws as possible by the time you're filling all your tables in a single service.

Slower trade should have been built into your initial forecasting, but once you've opened and you start to get a rough idea of average trade you can make gradual adjustments to your figures. This should help you when it comes to ordering stock and ingredients as you won't really have had an accurate idea of the amount and frequency to order things until you've opened.

While trade is slower this may be a good opportunity to bring in some of your marketing skills. Think about the different kinds of special offers you can introduce to try and boost trade. The *Ongoing Marketing* chapter gives you far more detail on this but it's something to consider during your early stages of trading. It can be difficult to get a lot of press coverage before you've opened, but now that you've got a menu to showcase, get yourself out there. Talk to the press, and if necessary, advertise in the local papers. At the opposite end of the spectrum, you should also be prepared for a massive influx of curious passers-by when you open.

TIP

You may not want to contract in lots of staff if you're not expecting a full house, but during your first few weeks of trading, ask a couple of your staff if they're happy to go on stand-by should you have an unexpectedly busy night. This only works if they live locally, but it can be really useful to have an extra kitchen porter or waiter you can call on at short notice.

IN MY EXPERIENCE:

Geetie Singh, The Duke of Cambridge

'On the first day we opened we served about 30 people. We had only budgeted for five. We broke even in our fourth month which is pretty extraordinary. However, that was partly because we weren't taking any money out of it ourselves. But we didn't really need any money. We were working the whole time, and eating and drinking at the pub.'

Difficult customers

The very best restaurants get it wrong sometimes so you can expect a few mistakes when you first open. Messing up somebody's order, making them wait 20 minutes for a drink, forgetting when they've asked for the bill – these things leave a first impression and if you've no other track record to go on, that's the word-of-mouth message that will get sent out when a disgruntled diner leaves the restaurant.

Not all your unhappy diners will tell you they're not satisfied. The trouble is, they'll probably tell their friends and family. It's for this reason you need to try wherever possible to recognise the signs that a diner is not enjoying their experience in your restaurant.

Look out for customers that seem agitated or are moving around a lot at their table. They may be trying to get attention without actually calling a waiter over. Politely ask if they would like anything, and if they're waiting for something, give them an estimation of when it's likely to arrive.

If a diner has left most of the food on their plate, don't interrogate them, but casually ask if they were unhappy with their meal. It may be that they simply weren't hungry enough to finish it, but if there was a problem with it, offer something as compensation – a free coffee perhaps. If there's a serious issue with the meal take it off the bill completely.

>
> **TIP**
>
> If you feel a customer is unjustified in their complaint, it's very important you remain calm when talking to them. Raising your voice or completely dismissing their claim will not do you any favours and may attract unwanted attention from other diners.

The customer may not always be right, but you'll still end up looking bad if you don't do all you can to try to assuage their dissatisfaction. Check out the *Getting Legal* chapter for more information on a customer's right to refuse to pay.

> **IN MY EXPERIENCE:**
> ## Shevonne Bennett, Brown Sugar
>
> 'At first we took a customer is always right approach, but we soon found that most of the customers complaining were still coming back to the restaurant anyway. I used to take complaints really personally but you soon realise not to take them to heart.'

Critics

The idea of a critic in your restaurant may seem daunting but you won't make a name for yourself unless the people that write about restaurants pay you a visit. There's detail on getting into the various restaurant guide books in *Ongoing Marketing*, but the likes of *Harden's* and *The Good Food Guide* aren't the only publications that send critics. Newspapers, magazines, local guides and websites can also decide to send a reviewer round to your new restaurant. First of all, view this as some assurance that your marketing is working. People know that you're open and find the concept of your restaurant interesting enough to check it out.

If you truly believe in the quality of your restaurant, you should have enough confidence to welcome a critic on any day of the week. If you feel you're not ready for the critics then you need to ask yourself why, and start making the appropriate changes immediately. Bear in mind too that a critic is not simply there to review the food. They'll want to see excellent service, and have a comfortable and pleasant dining experience.

You won't always know when a critic arrives at your restaurant so there's no point planning a special kind of service for when they do come. *The Good Food Guide* prides itself on all its inspections being entirely anonymous and paid for. And, even if a critic has announced their arrival, they'll be used to restaurateurs bending over backwards to please them, and they may well choose to observe how your treat your other customers rather than focus on their own reception.

However, gone are the days when the respected and well-established newspaper critic was the only one with the power to make or break the reputation of your restaurant. Online user-generated content means anyone can publish their views on your establishment. Websites like Toptable.co.uk are well read and can hugely influence your restaurant's reputation.

 TIP

If you want a thorough review of your own restaurant so that you can really judge where its weaknesses lie, why not enlist your own anonymous inspectors? Get a friend or family member that none of your staff know to come along to the restaurant and pretend to be a customer. They'll be able to report back on service and food quality from the point of view of a regular customer and may pick up areas of concern that you weren't aware of.

➡ ADAPTING YOUR IDEA

Assessing what works

 IN MY EXPERIENCE:
Ian Pengelley, Gilgamesh

'You're always going to have problems when you start but there's a point at which you say, that's enough now. What's not working? Do we need new managers? You need to be constantly checking everything. If you stay in the kitchen you'll never find out where all the problems lie. You have to get out and talk to your customers.'

Your first six months should be a constant process of assessing, recalculating and adjusting your forecasting, staffing needs and how much and how often you need to order stock. However, you've also got to consider whether the concept you've created for your restaurant is successful. To a certain extent this will be reflected in your figures. Are you meeting your sales forecasts? Are your outgoings in line with your income? But the bottom line doesn't necessarily give a true reflection of how well your concept is working at this early stage.

For one thing, you probably aren't making a profit yet. That's to be expected in a business where your initial costs are huge in comparison with the price of the items you sell. It may take months or even years to get back in the black after you launch, but that doesn't mean your restaurant isn't successful. It just takes time to recoup your investment.

However, another reason why your initial figures may not be a true reflection of how successful your concept has been is they may not reflect how satisfied your customers are. Even a restaurant that serves bad food can have a busy first few months, riding solely off the back of the curiosity of the locals at seeing a new place to try. The real measure is whether your customers are returning three, four or six months after opening. There are certain situations where most of your customers will be one-off diners, such as in tourist hotspots. However, in a residential area away from the centre of town, you'll go out of business very quickly if you can't get people to come back. So even if your restaurant is full every night for the first two months, have a look at who's filling it. Are you seeing the same faces again and again? If you are, then you've obviously been successful. If not, then you need to ask yourself why, and start thinking of ways to adapt your idea to get people to come back.

FROM THE EXPERTS:
Simon Kossoff, Carluccio's

'We opened in November 1999, and were immediately very busy at lunchtimes but not at any other time. We were also too cheap so weren't making any money. Despite having a good run up to Christmas it was clear to us we had to change the model, so we had to reinvent it. We made it more like a restaurant than a cafeteria.'

New ideas/trends

It's important to keep up with the latest food trends, but there's far more to this than avoiding prawn cocktail on your starters list. Food trends are as prone to fashion as the catwalk. Someone who writes more than they read makes for a bad author. Apply the same lesson to your restaurant. Make sure you eat out as much as you can in a wide variety of restaurants, so that you can pick up on new trends and ideas. The same applies for food shows and exhibitions. You never know where you'll pick up new inspiration.

TIP

Don't get too carried away or influenced by food fashion though. Let your taste and the experience of your chef ultimately determine what goes on the menu, or you may look back and wonder why on earth you paired such unlikely ingredients together in the name of a current trend.

The same goes for how your restaurant is run. You need to strike a balance between the current trends in dining experiences and what works for your style of restaurant. For example, there are quite a few eateries such as the hugely popular Gourmet Burger Kitchen which has adopted the style of a fast food restaurant, asking customers to pay at the point of ordering. This works well in this instance because of the style of cuisine and the casual ambience of the restaurant. Try it in your sophisticated French venue and you'll get a less than welcome response.

Updating your menu

There are plenty of good reasons to change your menu regularly. The first is that people get bored. This is particularly important if you have a small menu. During your first few months of trading you should keep an open mind about what goes on your menu. Returning customers are likely to try new things but you won't be able to determine what the favourite offerings on the menu are until several months in.

Once you've established what the favourites are, keep them there. You can still achieve variety while keeping your core popular dishes. There's nothing more frustrating for a regular customer than to arrive at a restaurant looking forward to a particular dish only to find it's been taken off the menu. Likewise, your regulars don't want to see exactly the same line up week in, week out.

Give all your dishes a chance, but don't keep something that never gets ordered on the menu just because it's your personal favourite. Try to identify why it's not popular. It could be as simple as the price. If that's the case, try it out at a lower price, but don't leave yourself out of pocket. If it's not working, the simplest solution is to just replace it with something else. And there should be plenty of new ideas to choose from if you think about the seasonality of your dishes. Use ingredients that are in season at that time. Not only will it show you're making a conscious decision to think about sustainability, it will also work out cheaper to buy in season.

There's another really important aspect to changing your menu every now and then, and it has nothing to do with your customers or pricing. You need to keep you chef stimulated. He or she doesn't want to be cooking the same tired dishes for months on end. For satisfaction in the kitchen you need variety. Consult your chefs and let them have input in the final decisions. Giving them new things to cook every now and again will stop them running on autopilot which may lead to a reduction in quality. Remember, if your chef isn't passionate about what they're cooking, it'll be reflected on the plate.

Sample dishes

One way of testing out new ideas for a menu is to give away samples of certain dishes you're considering. If possible, try these out on regular customers. They'll be more familiar with your usual menu and can therefore give you better feedback. The very fact that they're regular customers means they like your menu and style of cooking so you can get a better reflection of whether they'd respond well to the additions to the choices on offer.

There are two ways of giving out samples for customers to test out. The first is to bring them a small portion alongside what they've already ordered. This should be enough for them to get a proper taste but not enough to distract them from what they chose to order themselves. The second option is to offer them the new dish before they order, explaining that if they're willing to offer feedback on the dish, it won't appear on their bill.

 **CASHFLOW**

Contingency budgets

Your first few months of trading are all about learning the ropes. There's only one certainty during this period – you will come across unexpected costs. Not until you've had at least two years of trading will you be able to accurately map out peaks and troughs. There may also be equipment you didn't realise you needed before opening and therefore haven't budgeted for. Things can go wrong with your premises at any time, requiring the call out of plumbers, electricians and builders. These occurrences cost money, and if you don't have spare cash in the bank to cover it, you can get the business and yourself into some serious debt.

FROM THE EXPERTS:
Robin Rowland, Yo! Sushi

'When I joined I knew I could grow the business but also knew it would have to go through some difficult times before it became profitable. In our case we had eight restaurants that weren't contributing, and four successful ones. My job was to unpick that, make the banks believe in the concept of adding others, and make sure we didn't go bust. It was the hardest thing I've ever done in my life. There's no shortcuts with restaurants. It's a marathon, not a sprint.'

Build room in your ongoing budgeting for unexpected costs. The bigger percentage of your turnover you can realistically put aside, the better. This can be difficult in the early stages of trading when every last penny already seems accounted for. However, constantly trying to survive by living dangerously close to your overdraft limit leaves you vulnerable.

Another important reason for holding back a little of your budget is you may not have accurately budgeted for the correct amount of average covers, which in turn would have affected your planning in other areas of the restaurant. For example, you may have budgeted to pay three waiting staff every night for a month and given them contracts to that effect. Your initial sales may not cover the cost of these salaries at the beginning but if your staff worked those shifts, you have to pay them regardless of how much revenue was brought in. The cash to pay them has to come from somewhere, and if it hasn't come from last week's trading, it'll feel less painful taking it out of a contingency budget than getting overdrawn as a result.

IN MY EXPERIENCE:
Eza Philippe Navaratnasingam, The Lounge

'In the beginning, 85% of our sales were from drinks, and I just had a few bar snacks on the menu. But one-by-one more bars started to open up in the area and we started to lose business. We had to make some changes, so I added about 20 tapas items to the menu. But we were still losing money and I had to make a decision – quit or completely refurbish the place, changing it into a full restaurant. As soon as we did that, the food sales started to go up and the profits started to increase. I introduced 40 items to the tapas menu and replaced the chef.'

Adjusting pricing

Analysing your pricing should be an ongoing process. When you first start trading you'll need to do this with all your dishes. However, even when you've been open a few years you'll need to do the same analysis with all new additions to the menu. When you come up with a price for a dish such as lasagne you don't just price up the cost of the pasta sheets or the meat included. There's a measure of seasoning to be taken into account, the oil used in the pan and the gas or electricity required to cook it. These aren't things you necessarily have an accurate measure of before you start cooking the dish in large quantities on a regular basis.

By dividing the cost of the ingredients, energy and staff time by exactly how many covers you served with them, which is something you can only do once you've served enough of that particular dish, you can get a better reading of how much each dish actually costs to make. Once you have this accurate reflection of how much dishes actually cost you'll be able to adjust how much you charge for them, or even asses whether it's cost-effective to serve them at all.

There's more on menu pricing in the chapter *Managing the Books*.

 # OPENING HOURS AND SEASONS

Seasonal variations

There are obvious peaks and troughs which you can predict such as Fridays and Saturdays being busier than an average Tuesday. However, seasonal variations are a bit trickier. A great restaurant in a great location will be busy all year round but others rely on specific seasons for more trade. For example, if you've got outside seating, you can expect a larger turnover during the summer months. Not only will more diners be attracted to the fact they can dine al fresco, but you'll also increase the capacity of your restaurant.

 IN MY EXPERIENCE:
Eza Philippe Navaratnasingam, The Lounge

'I don't like it when it's too hot or sunny outside because we have less trade. Our busiest trade is on Friday and Saturday when we're full. Because of our capacity we can't really increase our turnover much more during that time. However, I'm always looking at ways to try and get more people in during the week.'

Special days

There are a few periods throughout the year you should pay particular attention to and make sure you're prepared for a sudden influx of customers by having extra staff on call, and by preparing your suppliers for additional, larger or more frequent orders. These are:

Christmas

The run up to Christmas is traditionally the time restaurants see the biggest amount of group bookings as offices make plans for their festive celebrations. You should prepare whoever takes bookings for this and make sure you've arranged a procedure for group bookings. Establish what the maximum party size you're willing to accept is. Are you prepared to hire the entire restaurant out to private parties on certain nights of the week? You should also prepare a set menu for large groups. It'll make serving large parties at the same time a lot easier on you, and is often preferred by customers as it makes it easier to budget how much the meal will cost.

Valentine's Day

Unlike the Christmas season this is certainly not a night to expect a lot of group bookings. The busiest night of the year for most restaurants, Valentine's Day is another night you may want to arrange a special menu for. You should organise this at least a month in advance as you can expect bookings and menu enquires well ahead of the actual day. You'll also need to make sure you rearrange your seating if your restaurant is made up of lots of larger party tables. This may not be possible if you have fixed tables or booths but is definitely something to consider if your seating arrangement is flexible.

Mothers' Day

This is another traditionally busy day for many restaurants. Again you'll want to arrange a special menu, although the focus will probably be more on a lunchtime service. You'll need a bigger variety of seating arrangements than Valentine's Day as you should expect bigger family parties.

Opening hours

Your opening hours should be a balance between what your customers are looking for and when you are your staff can realistically work. Once you've been open a while you'll have a better understanding of which days or periods are most cost-effective to open on. If you're getting virtually no diners on a Monday evening, or during weekday lunchtimes, you should work out if it's even cost-effective to pay all the staff you need to open at these times.

Likewise, if you've decided not to open at lunchtimes but other restaurants in the area are doing a roaring trade in the middle of the day, then it might be time to consider following suit, even if it means a bit of extra recruiting. It's all about trial and error. See what works and what doesn't, and remember that there's nothing to stop you starting or axing a service on a particular day or time.

Things to remember:

- Don't expect a stampede of customers at first. Use a slower build up of trade as an opportunity to hone your operation.

- Keep an eye on your menu, changing it as and when you feel a fresh update is needed, but be sure not to get rid of the most popular dishes even if you're bored with them.

- Always try and hold a little cash in the bank back for emergencies.

- Make sure you're prepared for busy periods such as Christmas, Valentine's Day and Mother's Day.

Finance 2: Managing the books

N ow comes the part least connected with serving great food and entertaining your customers – the financial side. You'll already have familiarised yourself with projections, forecasts and basic costings during the planning stage, but the reality of running any business is you need a firm grip on the numbers at all times.

In this chapter we'll go through what type of records you need to keep, covering both the financial and management categories. We'll also outline the role of cashflow in your business and what type of VAT you will be required to pay. Now that your business is up and running you'll need to be aware of the daily financial issues of running that business, such as price changes, accepting payments and the all-important task of depositing your takings at the bank. You'll need to decide what accounting system you will use, and whether you'll be keeping records yourself or hiring the services of an accountant. You may not find it fun, but getting it right is essential.

In this chapter we'll cover:

- Accounts
- Balance sheets
- Profit and loss sheets
- Cashflow forecasting
- VAT
- Price changes
- Managing payments
- Hiring an accountant
- Paying your staff

➡ ACCOUNTS

Running a business involves meticulous record keeping, some of which you are obliged to do, and some of which simply helps you run your business more efficiently. Your accounts can be separated into two main categories: financial and management.

Financial

If your business is incorporated, ie a limited company, you are required by law to put together a set of financial records every year and file them with Companies House. Unincorporated businesses are not required to do this but they must still keep thorough accounting records to be used alongside their annual tax returns. You are obligated to keep a minimum of the last six years' worth of accounts for HMRC to call upon at any time.

There are detailed guidelines for how to prepare financial accounts on the Companies House website at www.companieshouse.gov.uk, but you will generally have to include the following:

- Balance sheet
- Profit and loss account
- Cashflow statement

IN MY EXPERIENCE:

Eza Philippe Navaratnasingam, The Lounge

'I'd done bookkeeping as part of my roles in other restaurants in Switzerland and had accounts in my family so that side of things has never been too much of a problem for me. When I started I had an accountant who did things like payroll and VAT calculations. However, after my first year I wanted to cut costs so started doing it all myself after getting to grips with the UK system. Now I do 95% of it myself and give it to an accountant to check over at the end of the year.'

Management

Your management accounts are the records you must keep in order to run your business well. Here's where you'll cover everything from how many glasses of wine you served to how much your staff are due to be paid. You simply cannot run your restaurant efficiently without up-to-date and painstakingly methodical records.

What records do you need to keep when running a restaurant business? Well, your accounting records will be split into daily, weekly, monthly and annual figures, all of which are important. Efficient records will allow you to identify the strong and weak areas of your business and therefore take appropriate action in your day-to-day management and long-term planning.

Records you should keep to have an accurate reflection of your restaurant's financial health include:

- Customer transactions – including how may covers there were and which dishes and drinks were ordered
- Stock levels – daily, weekly and monthly
- Receipts both for cash and credit card transactions
- Invoices from suppliers and service providers
- Staff shifts and wages
- Cost of other overheads including premises and utilities

Balance sheet

Essentially, reading a balance sheet is like checking your bank balance on a monthly basis – it simply tells you what the business owes or owns at any particular time. But unlike your bank balance it doesn't just give you a number it also tells you what makes up that number. In essence it is everything your business owns – its assets. The second part is everything you owe – the liabilities.

The first part of the balance sheet should give you a figure that shows you the net worth of your business. That figure should also show in the second part of the business – also the net worth but working back from what capital you started with, any profits you have made and kept in the business or any money that you have taken out.

Here's a detailed explanation of all the sections of a balance sheet:

- Fixed assets – this is typically anything that you count as an asset of the business but not something that you are likely to sell as part of your daily business. So include any premises, vans or other vehicles you use for delivery, equipment or furniture that you use for the business.
- Current assets – anything that you sell or serve.
- Stocks – it's probably worth separating your currently assets into raw ingredients and ready-to-sell items such as drinks. The reason for this is that the cost of raw ingredients doesn't take into account how much they are worth when sold on a menu, whereas the value of a bottle of wine is more transparent.
- Debtors – anyone that owes you money should be included in here. Perhaps some regular customers will have a tab, or if you have corporate clients which entertain staff or associates in your restaurant, they may not pay in the same way as regular diners with a simple bill at the end of their meal.
- Current liabilities – anything that you owe that is payable within one year. In our list we have included creditors – which might include your suppliers as you will typically pay them in around 30 days – and the overdraft as this is probably repayable on demand.
- Net current assets – this is simply the sum of your current assets and liabilities both of which are likely to be under one year in lifespan. This is quite a useful figure to calculate as it will show whether you could pay all your debts if you collected all the sums due to you.
- Total Assets less Current Liabilities – unlike the last number you can include all the long-term assets like property in this number.
- Equity – any money that is invested in the business, for example your savings if you used those to set up the business initially.

IN MY EXPERIENCE:

Shevonne Bennett, Brown Sugar

'My projections for turnover were very accurate in terms of what we would bring in. However, I wasn't so spot on with my outgoings. A lot of unexpected things cropped up and I think my contingency planning could have been a lot tighter.'

Profit and Loss (P&L) sheet

Put simply, a profit and loss sheet details your business transactions, subtracting the total outgoings from the total income to give you a reading of how much, if any, profit you have made.

If your company is incorporated, you are required by law to produce a profit and loss sheet for each financial year. If your restaurant is not trading as a limited company you don't have to produce one, but the information you give to HMRC to work out your tax bill will amount to the same thing anyway. Even if you're not required to produce one, the P&L sheet is useful to show owners, investors and shareholders how the business is doing at a glance.

> ## ✦ TIP
>
> A profit and loss sheet, unlike a balance sheet, displays the financial health of your company for a period of time – a month, a quarter or a year. A balance sheet only represents your finances at a particular moment in time.

You can find an example restaurant P&L sheet at the back of this book on page 246.

Cashflow statement

A cashflow statement shows your restaurant's incoming and outgoing money, enabling you to assess how much money you have at your disposal at any one time. Poor cashflow is one of the number one causes for businesses to fail. Some businesses can be profitable on paper, earning more than their outgoings, but if the cash isn't in the bank to buy stock and the pay staff you'll soon find yourself in trouble. It's an issue restaurants are less at risk of getting into trouble with however, because of the nature of how they are paid by their customers – ie instantly after receiving service.

Having said that however, your first few months are the time you're most likely to run into difficulties with cashflow. A lot more money will have been spent by you – on premises, initial stock, equipment, staff – than the first few customers will pay you for their meals. There are certain things businesses can do to increase their cashflow and the most obvious is to ask their customers to pay them quicker. Restaurants can't really do that but here's a few things you can do to improve cashflow:

- Lease rather than buy the really expensive equipment you need. You'll then pay a monthly or annual charge rather than having to splash out all at once.
- Order less stock – Don't order too many of the items that will sit in your stockroom at once. Some long-life ingredients can be bought weekly instead of a bulk monthly buy. Buy less of your really high-end wines at once. They won't sell as quickly, and that could be cash earning interest in the bank instead of sitting in your wine cellar.
- Make sure you forecast your cashflow as accurately as you can. That way you can plan ahead for slower revenue periods and make sure you still have enough cash in the bank to cover your outgoings.

Cashflow forecasting

Good cashflow forecasting isn't just important for your own business management. You may be required to provide this kind of detail if you need a loan from the bank during your first few months of trading. The forecast will allow you to identify the amount and origin of cash coming into your business and the amount and destination of cash being paid out during any given period of time.

Generally you'll produce a forecast for a quarter or year in advance, but during the early stages of trading you might want to do this more frequently, such as a month in advance. When compiling a cashflow forecast it's really important that you don't overestimate your incoming cash.

TIP

It's much easier to get an accurate reflection of your outgoings as you will know what these are at this stage. However, you won't yet have a really accurate estimate of how many customers you'll have each month, so err on the side of caution to be safe and keep your incoming cash estimates low.

There is an example of a cashflow forecast sheet on page 245.

VAT

VAT or Value Added Tax applies to the majority of transactions involving the sale of goods or services. Once your business reaches a certain level of turnover, currently £67,000 per year, you are legally obliged to register for VAT. You will then have to apply VAT to what you sell and keep records of your incomings and outgoings in order to pay the correct amount of VAT to HMRC.

To register for VAT go to the VAT Online Registration Service on the HMRC website (www.hmrc.gov.uk).

There are three rates of VAT:

1. The standard rate: 17.5%
2. The reduced rate: 5%
3. The zero rate: 0%

Although most food sold in shops or market stalls is exempt from VAT, food served in, or taken away from, restaurants is not, and the standard rate of 17.5% applies.

It's really important you register for VAT in good time because you will liable for all VAT due from the time that you should have been registered. In other words you have to pay HMRC the right amount of VAT even if you didn't charge your customers for it. You could also be liable to pay a fine for delaying your registration. How much you'll be fined is dependent on how late you registered, but fines start at £50.

> ## TIP
>
> If you find the prospect of dealing with VAT daunting don't worry. You can appoint an agent – accountant, bookkeeper or tax advisor – to deal with it on your behalf by registering them on HMRC's VAT Online Registration Service.

The average time for processing VAT applications is about one month. However, it can take up to six months if HMRC feels it needs to carry out extra checks on the application. You must account for and pay VAT between applying for your registration and receiving your actual VAT number, but you are also allowed to reclaim any VAT you have paid suppliers on your purchases during this point. To do this you need to keep accurate records of any invoices where your suppliers have charged you VAT.

THE DAY-TO-DAY

Price changes

The cost of your outgoings will change, sometimes on a weekly basis. The price of ingredients and the cost of energy are variable and may go up at a faster rate, and more frequently, than you can realistically reprint your menus. While customers accept inflation as a fact of life, they'll start to cry foul play if the their favourite dish has gone up by a pound each time they order it. Consequently you need to find a balance between covering your own costs and maintaining reasonable prices on your menus.

One way of doing this is to set yourself a variable acceptable markup on food. For example, calculate what the lowest possible markup for an acceptable return is (eg 60%) then the highest mark-up you can reasonably expect to charge (70%). This gives you some leeway for price changes for your own costings without leaving you out of pocket for not passing the cost on to your customers. However, when your own costs go up so much that it's no longer possible to make at least the 60% markup, that's when you'll need to change your menu prices.

Here's an example of how markups work:

If you sell a steak at £10 and it only costs £6 to make, that's a 70% markup. However, if the price of ingredients, fuel, staff etc. go up and it then costs £6.50 to make, you'll only be left with a 55% markup. You'll then have to put your prices up to £10.50 to achieve a 60% markup.

Managing cash payments

Although you'll want to retain some cash from each service to make up the next till float, it's not a good idea to keep lots of cash on the premises, especially if you don't have a secure safe within the restaurant. However, your evening service will end long after the banks shut so you'll need to make some provision for storing cash safely before you can deposit it. Rooms where cash is stored should be as far away as possible from restaurant exits. If you do have a safe it's a good idea to have it fitted to the floor or within a wall.

> ### TIP
> Try not to go more than a day without taking cash to the bank, but avoid making deposits at the same time each day. Also, it's important to vary your route so you don't become an easy target for thieves that see you walking to the bank regularly.

The float

A lot of your customers will pay with plastic (credit or debit cards) and we've covered that in more detail in *Getting Legal*. However, some people still pay for their meals in cash, even in large amounts. As a result you need to make sure you have a float for each service so that change can be given out. It's a good idea to keep at least £100 in various notes, including as many £5 notes as possible. These can be hard to come by and are given out in change more than you're likely to receive them. You may find you need to get some from the bank if you don't have a large enough supply. You'll also need plenty of pound coins and smaller denominations as you're likely to give some change back with nearly every cash payment.

Cheque and credit card payments

Cheques are still used by some, but many businesses are now refusing to accept them for a number of reasons. Firstly, they generally take longer to clear than credit card payments, which can have an adverse affect on your cashflow. Secondly, there's no instant notification about whether the payment has been accepted, and unless your customer has used a cheque guarantee card, you may find yourself with the odd bounced cheque.

Credit and debit card payments will probably be the most popular way your customers pay for their meals but you need to be meticulous about your record keeping and storing of receipts. It'll cost you between 2% and 6% to accept a credit card payment. This will vary according to your bank and merchant account. For more information on setting up credit card payments for your restaurant, go back to *Getting Legal*.

IN MY EXPERIENCE:
Shevonne Bennett, Brown Sugar

'It can be hard to initially get merchant account status when you don't have any trading history, but once you sort it out, it's all very simple. We signed up with a company and got our chip and pin machines, which then made payments straightforward.'

ACCOUNTANTS

Even some of the most mathematically minded entrepreneurs will tell you a good accountant can be worth their weight in gold. You're a restaurateur, so the chances are you don't want to get bogged down with invoices, PAYE slips and credit notes. Handing that responsibility over to an accountant or someone who completely manages your books can free up your time to spend on planning, development and working on your grand designs for the future of your restaurant.

Choosing an accountant

When you're just starting out, your accountant can act as one of your most valued business advisors so you need to make sure you employ one that you trust. There are many ways to find a good accountant and one of the best methods is through a recommendation. Ask friends and contacts if they would recommend their accountant. Also ask businesses around you if they go to someone locally.

 TIP

Your solicitor or bank manager may also be able to recommend someone, or if not a particular person they should be able to point you in the right direction for an accountancy firm that specialises in the restaurant industry.

When seeking recommendations, make sure you ask people what they used their accountant for as you might not need the same kind of service. Ask what in particular they recommend about them and what their weak points are if they have any. Most importantly it is advisable to choose someone who is a member of one of the main professional accounting bodies. There is no legislation to stop anyone setting up as an accountant so asking for member accountants in your area will ensure you are getting someone fully qualified.

These are the main accounting organisations in the UK:

Association of Chartered Certified Accountants
Tel: 020 7059 5000
www.acca.org.uk

Institute of Chartered Accountants, Scotland
Tel: 0131 347 0100
www.icas.org.uk

Institute of Chartered Accountants, England and Wales
Tel: 020 7920 8100
www.icaew.co.uk

Where possible, choose an accountant familiar with the restaurant industry as they will be more familiar with the specific legislation that applies to you. Remember too that you're likely to be working closely with your accountant and if you don't get on at a basic level, your professional relationship may be more difficult than it needs to be. If you find someone you think you like ask if you can speak to their other clients. This is like asking for references and will be a real test of the calibre of the firm or individual accountant. If they are confident that their service has impressed, they shouldn't have a problem referring you to a few people.

IN MY EXPERIENCE:
Shevonne Bennett, Brown Sugar

'We hired an accountant early on but found out further down the line that they were actually rubbish. There are a lot of accountants out there who'll make out they can give you a great all-round service but don't really know what they're talking about. It's one area where it's definitely worth paying a premium price for a superior service.'

Accounting software

If you decide you're going to manage the books yourself you'll want to get some accountancy software. Whoever's job it is, yours or an accountant's, the person balancing the books, chasing invoices, managing suppliers and paying staff doesn't need to be worrying about the latest technology and it's probably the last thing on their mind. However, buying an accountancy software package can slash the amount of time and effort you put into managing your finances.

From reminders for chasing payment to generating invoices, a good package is like a virtual accounts department. It can tell you how much you are owed and by whom; how long it takes you to pay your bills; what you have in stock and what you have in the bank at any moment in time. More importantly, it could also give you those vital breakdowns of how much you are making on each service, day or month. Of course, there's nothing stopping you or your accountant working from a basic Excel spreadsheet, but bear in mind that a good accountancy software package can drastically reduce your accounting bill every year.

There are plenty of packages out there, each tailored to the size and type of business being run. You can also choose a package that links up to your EPoS system if you have one, which we have already covered in *Decking It Out*.

When choosing an accounting software package consider the following before you buy:

- Value for money – what services do you get for your buck?
- Level of support – does the package include a free helpline you can call for technical or set-up support?
- Is the software industry specific?
- Does it integrate easily with HMRC's online filing system? This can save you a lot of time when it comes to filing your returns.

➡ PAYING YOUR STAFF

Restaurants often have a lot of casual and temporary staff, and it can be tempting to just pay them cash at the end of each week or shift. However, it's your responsibility as an employer to make sure the payment of your staff is all above board and both they and your business are making the appropriate tax and National Insurance contributions.

PAYE

PAYE (Pay As You Earn) is HMRC's system for collecting income tax and National Insurance at the source of payment – ie before the employee receives it. It's your responsibility to make sure you know how much to deduct from your staff in terms of their personal tax requirements. You must send the deducted amounts to HMRC by the 19th of every month (or the 22nd if you make electronic payments). However, if monthly payments are under £1,500 you can do this on a quarterly basis.

You have three choices when it comes to organising PAYE. You can either keep written accounts and calculate tax and National Insurance deductions yourself, buy specialised software to help calculate it for you, or outsource the whole operation.

PAYE is applied to all payments your employees receive when working for you. This includes:

- Wages
- Overtime
- Tips
- Bonuses
- Statutory sick pay
- Statutory maternity / paternity / adoption pay
- Some lump sums including redundancy payments

Once again, a quick visit to the HMRC website will allow you to register your business for PAYE. You should have already done this before employing your first member of staff, but if you haven't done so already, give the HMRC's New Employer Hotline a call on 0845 60 70 143 and order a New Employer Starter Pack. This will talk you through the basics of registering.

Staff records

There are three main types of documentation you need to give your staff so they have a record of what they've earned and how much income tax and National Insurance they've paid. These are:

- Wage slips – this shows how much they've earned and how it has been calculated.
- P60 form – this shows the tax deducted during the whole tax year. You can order this from HMRC by calling the Employers Orderline on 0845 7646 646.
- P45 – you only need to give your employees this when they stop working for you. It will contain their individual tax code which they need to pass on to their new employer.

Outsourcing payroll

Many small businesses decide to outsource their payroll duties so they don't have to calculate tax and National Insurance deductions themselves. This will obviously be an added expense for your restaurant but can save you a lot of time and money in the long-run. By outsourcing your payroll you get rid of one of the biggest administrative headaches of running a small business.

IN MY EXPERIENCE:

Shevonne Bennett, Brown Sugar

'I did the payroll myself for the first couple of months but as our team got bigger I had to outsource it to another company.'

If you have an accountant, they should be able to provide you with advice on outsourcing your payroll, and may even by able to do it for you. As with any service, shop around for the best deal as much as time permits.

Before you decide on an outsourced payroll provider, make sure you consider the following:

- Are they used to dealing with restaurant businesses?
- Do they supply monthly or weekly pay slips? You may find weekly slips are more suited for casual staff.
- How much will they charge for setting up your payroll system?
- What are the ongoing fees?
- How easy is it to add extra members of staff to the account?
- Is the software they use approved by HMRC?

Things to remember:

- Be thorough in your record keeping. The better organised your figures are, the better your organised your restaurant will be.

- Be cautious in your forecasting. It's better to underestimate trade than expect a full house every night.

- Make sure you register for VAT in good time to avoid HMRC delays.

- Don't try to manage it all yourself if you don't have the time or skills. Hire an accountant if you need one.

- Consider outsourcing your payroll but carry out the appropriate checks before handing the process over to a third party.

Management of staff and yourself

There's simply no avoiding the fact that a restaurant is nothing without a great team of people in place. Strong and effective leadership must come from the top and filter down, which means you have to make sure you're an effective manager as well as ensuring your staff are well supervised. You need to be familiar with the qualities of effective leadership and how to motivate your staff. To make sure you have the best team possible in place at your restaurant you'll need to look at your own skills and faults, as well as those of your staff. This means taking account of how you spend your time in the restaurant and identifying when you can afford to take a well deserved break.

When evaluating your team of staff you'll have to consider not just problems like theft but also if they could benefit from any training or if there are any benefits you could offer to motivate them. Getting good staff doesn't end with recruitment, it's an ongoing process, so you may have to take active steps to reduce staff turnover and keep abreast of the myriad of HR legislation.

In this chapter we'll cover:

- How to manage yourself
- When to take advice
- Time management and holidays
- Employing a manager
- Managing staff
- Wages
- Dealing with HR problems
- Staff incentives

➡ MANAGING YOURSELF

Being a restaurateur is far more than having an eye for a good dish, or being a good host. You become a boss, a manager and the point from which authority and company culture flows.

Advice, mentors and role models

We covered the value of taking advice from others in *Before You Start,* but it's important to remember this is not something you should forget about once you're up and running. Mentors and established entrepreneurs can have something to offer your business even if it's a decade old. It's always good to have an outsider's perspective – they may be able to tell you where your strengths lie, and which areas of the business or management you're neglecting.

Once you've established yourself as a restaurateur you may find people more willing to confide and share with you as you can offer them advice in return. Networking should be an ongoing process. There are large organisations such as the British Hospitality Association (www.bha.org.uk) where you'll have access to other restaurateurs at events, but you should also consider the value of continuing to go to food industry trade shows and exhibitions.

IN MY EXPERIENCE:
Geetie Singh, The Duke of Cambridge

'I asked advice from other restaurateurs I had worked with and people I knew in the industry. Everyone was fantastically willing. I didn't meet anyone that didn't want to share information, but I was very upfront with them. I'd tell them I wasn't planning to open near or in competition to them. I've found that people are always willing to give advice because it's flattering. But I also turned up very well prepared, had well thought out questions and never argued. Since setting up my business a lot of people have asked for my advice, but I get really angry if they're vague and haven't thought things through first because that wastes my time.'

Also, don't rule out general free business networking events such as Startupslive, details of which can be found at www.startupslive.co.uk. These types of events bring together entrepreneurs from all kinds of industries, and you never know when a contact you make will come in useful. As a restaurateur you mustn't think that only other restaurateurs can offer useful advice or guidance. Running a restaurant shares the same principles of running any kind of business and you'll be surprised at how friendly and open to communication people can be when they share the same goals as you.

Identifying your strengths and weaknesses

As a business owner you develop and hone your skills everyday. However, if you want to maintain a successful business, you have to dedicate just as much time to your self-development as to your restaurant.

It can be hard to measure your own personal development when you're your own boss. Just because your restaurant turns over a tidy sum at the end of each month, doesn't mean you're as effective as you can be as a leader. That's where the focused and planned development of your knowledge and skills through training can benefit you.

Running a restaurant, much like running any other kind of small business, requires you to be multi-skilled. The role of restaurateur can involve everything from cooking and serving to marketing, business planning and taking care of the accounts. Regardless of whether you have a hands-on position in all of these rolls you need to at least be familiar with what they entail.

Watch your chefs; learn about the process of cooking certain dishes. Ask questions of your accountant. You may not be a whizz with numbers but you still need to understand the basics of a tax form. If you can't afford an army of experts to staff your restaurant with, then take advantage of the help available to you. Contact your local Regional Development Agency (www.englandsrdas.com), or visit a Business Link (www.businesslink.gov.uk) advisor. They can point you in the right direction to what's on offer in terms of training. Many courses are free for small business owners, so you can't even use lack of funds as an excuse.

The industry moves fast. What's en vogue for a menu or restaurant décor one month may seem passé half a year down the line. You need to keep up-to-date with the latest restaurant trends and fashions. Go to regular wine tastings and visit trade shows. You'll be surprised at what you can get out of them – new ideas, inspiration and a wealth of new contacts, possible suppliers or even customers.

Motivating yourself

The fact that you've even chosen to start a restaurant suggests you're an incredibly motivated person, but once the doors have opened and the regular customers start to flock, how can you make sure you maintain that level of enthusiasm? The start-up process is incredibly demanding both physically and psychologically. After all that hard work you clearly need to slow down the pace slightly, but you can't sit back and hope the restaurant will run itself.

Set yourself goals to work towards. Some of these will be on a weekly basis, but more long-term ambitions can do wonders for maintaining your motivation levels.

Time management

With so many hats to wear in your role as restaurateur, managing your time effectively could mean the difference between life or death for your business. It's absolutely critical that you grasp the principles of strong time management from a very early stage.

The most important aspect of time management is to prioritise everything you need to do. This will allow you to recognise the difference between what's important and what's urgent. Running a restaurant will involve various 'to do' lists. There's your long-term goals, such as growing turnover and improving your margins, nurturing and expanding your customer base and developing your own skills as a business owner.

Next come your monthly goals, which could involve developing a new menu, recruiting new waiting staff, getting your accounts in order. And of course there'll be daily and weekly objectives – running a successful service, testing out a deal or promotion, getting customers to try sample dishes.

If you are involved in the process of a service – food preparation, greeting diners – there will obviously be certain times of the day you can't focus your attention on administrative or planning responsibilities. Whatever your role within the actual restaurant opening times, you need to set aside enough time to get on with these tasks as they are just as important as serving customers when it comes to running a successful establishment.

Here are a few tips for prioritising workloads and making sure you don't neglect important aspects of running your business:

- List all the tasks you need to do, and then prioritise them in order of what is most urgent and important.
- Don't underestimate the amount of time interruptions can steal from your schedule. When allocating time for a particular task, build in room for disruptions.
- Don't be afraid to turn off your phone or email when you really need to concentrate. If having no distractions helps you get a task done more quickly, you may end up with extra time to deal with clients, customers or staff.
- Break large tasks up into manageable chunks. It's tempting to run lots of little errands instead of getting stuck in to a big important job. However, completing it one stage at a time will make it seem less daunting.
- Build room in your schedule for unexpected problems or events. If nothing unforeseen crops up, you'll end up ahead of schedule.
- Make sure no more than half your time is allocated to top priority work. All those little jobs that aren't as time sensitive will start to mount up if you don't crack on with them.
- If possible, delegate. You may think the business will fall apart if you don't oversee everything, but perhaps your time can be more valuably spent on other tasks.

Holidays and work/life balance

Deciding when the right time to take a break is a tricky thing to master. On the one hand your restaurant will still be very much in its infancy at this stage. However, you will have worked incredibly hard to get the venture up and running and may feel in desperate need of break by this point.

There's no specific right or wrong answer to when the best time to take a break or holiday is. At such an early stage in the company's life you may feel you simply can't afford to leave it in someone else's hands, even if you're desperate for a break. The main thing to remember is that you need a balance between working hard to make sure the restaurant thrives during its early days, and making sure you don't burn out yourself. Working too hard without a break can be counterproductive, and it's always best to take a breather before you get to the point where you simply can't keep up the pace.

If you do decide to take a break then test the waters first. Don't book two weeks in the sun without knowing for sure you've got a solid team in place to run things in your absence. Try handing over the reins for a weekend while you're still close at hand. That way you can test things are capable of running smoothly in your absence while still being nearby if any real problems arise.

Once you're confident the whole operation won't collapse as soon as you've closed the door behind you, you'll find you have a far more rewarding break and can come back refreshed, raring to go, and hopefully full of new ideas for the restaurant.

Handing over the reins

Employing a manager to run the restaurant for you is a big step. Whether or not you do this from the outset will probably depend on how big your restaurant is. A smaller establishment can get by with the roles of head chef and manager being fulfilled by you. However, It may not have been your intention to spend every evening working in the restaurant yourself, in which case you'll want to employ someone to run the restaurant for you, albeit with you still firmly in control of its direction and future.

Before you even think about hiring a manager, you must be sure it's what you really want. You'll have to delegate a lot of responsibility and you'll run into problems if you're not willing to relinquish some control and allow the manger to have a degree of autonomy.

Be clear in your head about why you've decided to take someone on in this role. Are you just looking for someone to watch over the restaurant when you're not there, or are you handing over more responsibility than that? Will they be completely in charge of hiring and firing other staff? How much input will they have when it comes to menu and pricing changes? What role do you still want to play, if any, in the day-to-day running of the business?

It's so important to have all this worked out before you start recruiting as it will determine the type of person you're looking for, how much you're willing to pay them and what kind of relationship they'll have with both you and the other members of staff.

➡ MANAGING STAFF

An efficient kitchen is a well-oiled machine. To run successfully, everyone must know their place. It's a highly pressured environment and, as a result, there must be discipline. You can't be afraid to assert your authority and you need to make sure your head chef or manager also has the confidence to direct staff with a strict but fair hand.

Kitchen authority

The different levels and ranks of authority will depend on the size of your kitchen and how many members of staff work in your restaurant. There's a more detailed explanation of the various kitchen roles in the *Recruiting Staff* chapter, but to summarise, the kitchen is the domain of the head chef. Whether that role is filled by you or someone you employ, the head chef must have good management skills. In a large kitchen your head chef has to rely on others, so will need to know, not only how to delegate, but also how to teach.

When in full swing trying to satisfy a dining room full of hungry customers, a restaurant is a hectic place to work. There must always be someone in charge, and it's up to you to put these systems in place. Make sure there's a clear level of command that all staff are aware of. That way if there are unexpected absences, it's always clear who's responsible for taking the reins.

Some restaurants with larger kitchens have regular staff meetings before every service. This doesn't have to be as formal as sitting round a table, but could just involve a quick gathering in the kitchen of both waiting and kitchen staff. This a good opportunity to brief staff on things such as what the specials are for that day, as well as offer constructive criticism or even praise for the previous service.

More formal and longer meetings should also be conducted at regular intervals to discuss things like menu changes or where any particular staff training is required. These less regular meetings are also a good opportunity to hear new ideas on menus, suggestions for deals or promotions or any other ideas members of staff may have come up with during the day-to-day running of the restaurant.

IN MY EXPERIENCE:
Eza Philippe Navaratnasingam, The Lounge

'When we started, things were working ok for a while but the quality was up and down with the chefs. The balance sheets were also not quite right and I couldn't tell if it was as a result of portion size, wastage or what. That's when I decided to get rid of the chef and take over the kitchen myself. I kicked the chefs out and took on some assistants instead. Now I don't hire chefs that are as experienced because I find it's harder to make them co-operate with exactly how I want things made.'

Staff training and courses

The restaurant industry is one where the most important techniques and principles are learned on the job. However, that doesn't mean you or your head chef should be left with the responsibility of teaching everything. For example, if none of your kitchen staff have a certificate in basic food hygiene, this is something you'll want to rectify as soon as possible. There are plenty of courses, most of which can be done in a day or less, which teach the fundamentals of avoiding food contamination.

The majority of prosecutions for poor kitchen quality are as a result of one individual being slack with hygiene or food preparation, so it's definitely worth investing in making sure you and your staff are up to speed on this issue. Don't wait until a problem arises before you get your staff adequately trained.

Why not dedicate a day where all, or at least half, the restaurant's staff can train together? This doesn't have to involve leaving the restaurant. Many courses involve a tutor or lecturer coming to you and doing on-site training.

FROM THE EXPERTS:
Simon Kossoff, Carluccio's

'Most people that come to work with us aren't looking for a career in the industry but that's what they end up with. The only problem is it's all very transitory. Not unlike a number of other companies, we put enormous effort into training our people. We have a training kitchen in our store in Islington where we do teaching every Friday. All our new chefs go to college one day a week to learn Italian food skills. I think it creates loyalty, and has reduced our staff turnover in that area.'

Wages

The restaurant trade is one which experiences staff turnover rates of 80% and above. If budgets allow, paying a competitive salary to your staff is one way of avoiding having to constantly recruit. If your staff are getting a better rate at your restaurant than nearby outlets, they have an incentive to stay.

To a certain extent you can choose how much you pay your staff. However, you must stick to the national minimum wage (NMW). This is the minimum amount per hour you can pay any person that works for you. The amount, which is regularly updated to take into account things like inflation, is set by the central government and there are tough penalties for not paying your staff in line with it, including risk of prosecution.

The restaurant trade in the UK has come under fire recently as several large chains were accused of not paying their staff the NMW. Many restaurateurs argued that by including tips or gratuity in the hourly rate, the total amount falls within or above the legal minimum. However, in June 2008, HMRC won a High Court battle with restaurant and night club chain Annabel's resulting in tips no longer being allowed to count as part of NMW.

This means that as long as tips are not paid directly through the employer's payroll system, the restaurateur must pay their staff minimum wage, which is currently £5.73 per hour for workers over the age of 22 (as of 1 October 2008). However, as previously mentioned, the NMW is constantly being revised and it's up to you to make sure you're aware of any changes. Check Startups.co.uk for the most up-to-date rate.

When you employ others it is also your responsibility to make sure you make appropriate National Insurance contributions on their behalf. See the Recruitings Staff chapter for more information on your tax and National Insurance obligations as an employer.

➡ DEALING WITH STAFFING PROBLEMS

Most employers will experience difficulties with certain members of staff at various points in their career. The restaurant trade has high levels of staff turnover so keeping hold of staff that you trust and who are dedicated and loyal to your business is no easy task. Unless you're extremely lucky, or only hire friends and family to work in the restaurant, it's likely you'll have to confront some of the following problems:

Theft

You're far more likely to come across light fingers in the stock room than to have to chase non-paying diners down the high street. Alcohol is also an easy target if staff think the odd missing bottle of wine will go unnoticed. There's also the threat of till thefts to contend with. Any business that deals largely in cash transactions could fall victim to staff theft. And it's your profit that's walking out of the door, not turnover. If somebody is taking £10 a day on a turnover of £1,000 that's only 1% and you might think you can live with that. But if you're pulling in 6% profit (£60) on that £1,000, then thieves are taking one sixth of your profits. These losses need to be seen as a percentage of net profit not of gross turnover.

Although common in the restaurant business, there are steps you can take to reduce the prevalence of staff theft. The best place to start is with recruitment. Even if you're only employing part-timers, check their references. It's the casual staff that you need to pay the most attention to.

The next step is to explain to all members of staff the security controls operating in your business. Make sure everybody knows what will happen to them if they're caught stealing, then at the very least they can evaluate the risks involved before they pilfer.

You should also ensure the lines of authority and responsibility are clearly defined – staff need to know who they're responsible to and for. That way you stand a much better chance of a member of your team confiding in you if somebody is stealing.

It may be a tedious task but you also have to put in place systems that will alert you to possible staff theft problems. For example, you should be able to average out cashflow and sales over a week and over a month. This allows you to build up a picture of how much you should be taking on a Monday in September, say.

It's also a good idea not to hold too much cash in tills as it can be a temptation. You only really need to carry enough cash to give change from a £50 note, all the surplus notes should be removed regularly.

What to do if you catch staff stealing

Once you're absolutely convinced you know which member of staff is stealing from you, it's then time to confront them. The simplest approach is to take them to one side and explain that you've discovered their theft and show them your proof. Unfortunately it's unlikely you'll even be able to trust someone again if you catch them stealing, and the best option for your own piece of mind may be to get rid of them. If you do decide to give them another chance however, make sure you give them a formal written warning which will make it easier to justify dismissal should the problem happen again.

Bad service, laziness and body language

Your restaurant may be a business to you, but for the people that eat in it, it's a place of entertainment and leisure. People go out to eat to socialise, have fun and often simply because they want to be served a meal in a pleasant and friendly environment without the hassle of cooking themselves. For that reason, you and your staff need to provide them with a pleasant dining experience.

If you're permanently positioned front of house, you'll be able to spot straightaway if your waiting staff aren't giving customers their full attention or diners are unhappy with the level of service they're receiving. Bad service can be enough to put customers off returning, even if their food was excellent. However, excellent service may be enough to encourage a return even if the food proves mediocre.

Encourage your staff to be enthusiastic but not too imposing. There's a fine line between being friendly and being annoying. Body language should reflect enthusiasm and a willingness to attend to diners as and when they need service.

Appearances are also important. If there's a uniform in place at the restaurant, make sure staff are changed into it before they walk past customers. If you don't require your staff to wear a uniform then make sure you set certain standards in the dress code from the outset. It can be difficult to tell people what they're wearing isn't suitable if you haven't given any guidance on clothing in the first place.

Discrimination

We've already touched on the issue of discrimination during the *Recruiting Staff* chapter but it's important to note this is something you must bear in mind constantly. There's plenty more detail on how to comply with discrimination laws on Startups.co.uk but to summarise, you must consider the following acts in the day-to-day running of your restaurant or you could find yourself in seriously hot water.

Legislation outlawing age discrimination came into force in 2006. It includes every member of staff that works for you, both young and old. Employers must have age-positive practices. This means you can't recruit, train, promote or retire people on the basis of age unless it can be objectively justified. Many people over 50 want to work but are prevented from doing so by ageist practices. But remember, the recent legislation doesn't just concern older people; it covers young and old alike throughout their working lives.

Skills, experience and the ability to do the job are what's important, not someone's age. However, the legislation doesn't just have advantages for employees. As a restaurateur, stamping out age discrimination can have a positive effect on staff turnover, higher morale, lower recruitment costs, better productivity and increased profits.

The same applies when it comes to discriminating on the grounds of race, sex or disability. It's your responsibility to make sure that not only do you treat all your staff equally, but that discrimination does not take place between other members of the team.

Discrimination can take many forms, and it's not just a case of refusing to hire someone for being a woman/gay/ 65 years old. There's also indirect discrimination, where certain members are denied opportunities within employment, harassment such as unwanted advances or comments of a sexual nature, or bullying.

If somebody working for you is a victim of any of these kinds of discrimination you could find yourself fighting in an employment tribunal, which is costly in terms of time, reputation and turnover.

Staff handbook

In an industry with such a high rate of staff turnover, you may have staff that only last a few months or even weeks at your restaurant. While you need to make sure every member of staff involved in food preparation has the appropriate training in food hygiene and health and safety, some of the other expectations of employee policy can be detailed in a staff handbook. Here you can list your expectations of all staff and your policy on issues such as theft, absence, dress code and general working attitude. That way if a problem ever arises you can refer back to the handbook as an explanation of why you may be taking disciplinary action.

However, you should also use the handbook as a way of flagging up staff benefits and the elements of your restaurant that you think are the advantages of working there.

> **What goes in a staff handbook?**
>
> Your staff handbook should cover your policy on:
>
> - Company morals or ethos
> - Dress code
> - Dealing with customers
> - Absence and lateness procedure
> - What day of the week or month salaries are paid
> - Holiday entitlement
> - Any bonus or reward schemes
> - Health and safety procedures

Staff benefits

Thinking about the extra perks which can make your restaurant stand out as a great place to work compared to the many other establishments your staff may have experienced can reduce your staff turnover.

Here are a few examples of the kind of things you can do for staff to encourage loyalty and hard work:

- Provide them with meals either at the start or end of their shift
- Offer bonuses or gifts for staff that never miss a shift or turn up late, or just generally as a reward for hard work and enthusiasm
- Celebrate birthdays or special occasions – this could be in the form of a toast or even something as simple a card signed by all the other members of the team.
- Offer extra benefits for long-term service. Offering an extra day's holiday per year of service can be far more cost-effective then going through a recruitment process for a head chef or manger every couple of months.
- Offer regular appraisals and give staff the opportunity to discuss any issues they want to raise. There may not be time during normal shifts to talk about problems or ask questions. Make sure you're approachable when staff really need you to listen.

FROM THE EXPERTS:
Iqbal Wahhab, The Cinnamon Club and Roast

'At our first staff Christmas party at The Cinnamon Club one of the waiters made a toast and said: "We're working really hard to make your dream come true". But this upset me a bit because I wanted them to be working towards their own dreams too. It's not just about your own indulgence; it needs to give them satisfaction too. So I did things like have my staff go through the dining experience in the restaurant themselves. For a lot of them, even with a discount it's still out of their league to pay for that kind of meal. But it's important they experience it from the other side too.'

Things to remember:

- Take advice as and when you need it, whatever stage in your restaurant career you're at.

- Set goals for effective time management, taking breaks when you need them.

- Learn to delegate. You can't do everything on your own.

- Be fair but authoritative, and make sure all your managers and chefs do the same.

- Reward good work wherever possible. An atmosphere where staff are only singled out when they do something wrong breeds bad morale.

Ongoing marketing

Y ou've overcome the first hurdle by getting those first few customers through the door. Perhaps you hosted an extravagant launch party that made the local papers, or got a few celebrity guests to draw attention to your first night's service. The tricky process is making sure you stay in the forefront of your customers' minds. It's no good if they come in for one meal, leave relatively impressed then don't come back again. You want repeat custom, and a constant supply of brand new customers too. This is where your ongoing marketing comes in.

This chapter will help you determine what your marketing plan should be and what kinds of marketing work best for you. This could include promotions to help increase business in those problem areas such as an offer at lunchtime or an early-bird discount. There is also advice on how to get your restaurant into a variety of listings and guides so your customers know what you offer and where to find you.

In this chapter we'll cover:

- What marketing is
- How to form your own marketing strategy
- How to measure the success of your marketing plan
- Ideas for offers and promotions

- Advertising and public relations (PR)
- Getting into restaurant guides and business directories
- How to market your business online

➡ WHAT IS MARKETING?

Marketing is the means by which your business identifies, anticipates and then satisfies customer demand. If carried out effectively it will not only ensure that your restaurant is seen and heard but it will also give it the flexibility to adapt to changing customer demands and an ever-evolving business environment.

Restaurants that really succeed are those where the owner has a vision for the firm and is dedicated to seeing it through. Marketing will help you understand who your potential diners are, place and price the product compared to the competition and also position the company in the market place. It will also help identify future opportunities for self-promotion.

Though there are established guidelines to follow, marketing is more of an art than a science and is a difficult skill to develop. But in terms of a successful impact on the future commercial effectiveness of the business, it is worth cultivating. It can offer improved returns and profitability and a greater understanding of realistic business development opportunities.

One of the major problems for restaurateurs when considering marketing is quantifying in advance the expected result for a given spend. But you should never underestimate the power effective marketing can have in terms of making your restaurant a success. Take one of the biggest companies in the world as an example – Microsoft. While your ambitions may be more modest than those of Bill Gates, his company's domination of the software industry is a testament to the power of successful marketing.

Gates targeted potential customers by undercutting bitter rival, Apple Computers, and at the same time launching a sustained marketing blitz. Today, despite Apple having made significant progress in clawing back a large chunk of the market share, Gates is still one of the richest men in the world and the PC dominates the home computer market. Industry observers attribute Microsoft's success as much to its marketing as the quality or price of its products.

Marketing plans

There are no hard and fast rules for creating a marketing strategy. It's up to you to set your own goals. However, as general rule, you need to ask what you want the restaurant to achieve in a year, two years or even five years time compared to where it would be without a marketing strategy.

Here are some tips to remember when devising your marketing plan:

- Start by setting clear objectives – where do you want the restaurant to go?
- Define your target market and identify your potential customers.
- Decide on the brand and the values you want to communicate.
- Plan your promotion strategy.
- Set a budget.
- Devise a schedule.
- Decide how the strategy will be measured, for example, increased sales, direct responses, coverage in local press etc.
- Implement the programme according to the schedule.
- Monitor and evaluate results as an aid for future marketing decisions.

Measuring success

If you've got several marketing or PR strategies happening at once it can be difficult to measure which ones are actually bringing in the customers. You're not going to advertise in a newspaper and then ask each customer that walks through the door if they're dining in your establishment because they saw an advert in the local rag. If you're not sure which marketing technique is giving you the best return on investment then why not try them one by one, then calculate any increase in customers or turnover for that period.

Of course the success of certain promotions are easy enough to measure because you can count up how many customers make use of the offers. However it's important to remember that you need to bring in more custom as a result of the promotion than you spend on your marketing. It's no good offering discounted rates, or free bottles of wine if there are bums on seats but lower profit margins than a half full restaurant.

FROM THE EXPERTS:
Robin Rowland, Yo! Sushi

'I focus our marketing more at store level. The best way of doing that is through local PR and educating people about sushi and the innovation of our operation. It's hard to measure how successful it is though. We spend about 1% of our turnover on marketing and PR. Whether I get a return on that is very hard to tell for sure, but we've had sustained like-for-like growth for the last five years and some part of that must have been played by marketing.'

➡ PROMOTIONAL IDEAS

One way of attracting new customers is to run special offers or promotions on various days, times or for certain periods. Here are a few restaurant promotional ideas you can try in the restaurant:

Lunch offer

Although traditionally not as busy a time as the evening trade, there's still plenty of scope for a full restaurant during the lunchtime period. Consider a special menu at lunchtime which could consist of different items. You may also want to try a discounted rate for two courses, or a main and a drink.

Loyalty card

This is something that can be stamped or signed so that each time a customer visits they build up to something for free. It could be a free bottle of wine, main or dessert for every six visits. The main point is it gets your diners to come back regularly.

Free wine

You could try offering a free bottle of house wine in return for parties of a certain size, or perhaps to all diners that order a starter and a main on certain days of the week. If you choose to restrict this kind of offer to a particular day, do it on one of your slower days. You may find it fills more tables on traditionally slow Monday evenings.

FROM THE EXPERTS:
Simon Kossoff, Carluccio's

'We run promotions that look very local and individual, even if they've come from central office. I also make my personal email address available on the site and reply myself.'

Buy one get one free

The staple in any promotion diet. This type of offer is commonplace in retail outlets but there's no reason you can't introduce it to your restaurant. You may want to offer two main meals for the price of one on a certain night, at lunchtimes, or on presentation of a voucher. If you can't afford to offer a whole main meal for free, why not try the offer with a glass of wine, or perhaps dessert?

Early bird discounts

In much the same way as a lunchtime offer can attract customers during the quieter hours, a discounted rate for customers that dine before 7.30pm could provide the extra few covers you need to get your profit margins up.

Premium dishes

While discounting can attract a lot of new customers, adding a special edition to the menu can also generate a fair amount of interest. You may want to offer one dish with particularly rare or premium ingredients, or perhaps something so extravagant it has to be ordered well in advance. Not many people will order it, but if it gets tongues wagging, who cares?

FROM THE EXPERTS:
Iqbal Wahhab, The Cinnamon Club

'One day my chef came to me and said: "You know how you're always telling us we have to use the best ingredients? Well I've found this fantastic venison from Ireland I want to do a tandoori chop with pickle and spices with it." I asked him what the problem was and he told me we'd have to charge £28 to get any kind of markup on it. I looked at him and said: "Charge £31. Everyone will be so curious they'll order it." To this day, it's the most popular thing on The Cinnamon Club's menu. It's only my PR background that could produce that kind of thinking, so in the end, what some perceived to be a weakness became my biggest strength.'

➡ ADVERTISING VS PR

We've already discussed advertising in *The Opening*, but it's important to consider the value of continuing to advertise if you feel you're not reaching enough customers. While initial advertising campaigns are good for informing customers that may not walk past the restaurant of your presence, ongoing advertising can be great for flagging up promotions or seasonal menu changes. However, this early on in your restaurant's life, you may not yet be breaking even, let alone have enough profits set aside to spend on advertising. That's where PR can prove extremely useful.

IN MY EXPERIENCE:
Lisa Tse, Sweet Mandarin

'Since our book has come out we've started rebranding the menu so that we have specials that tie in with the book. Anyone that reads the book wants to try our food and it's already gone out to 33 countries. We've also started doing things like food and wine pairing evenings. As time goes on we are getting more and more savvy when it comes to marketing.'

You may have had coverage in a local paper or free magazine when you launched but how do you keep the PR momentum going once you've been open a few months? One way is to build a story around yourself or the restaurant. If you source all your ingredients ethically and want to publicise the fact that you run a green restaurant, send out a press release to some relevant publications.

Another interesting way of getting the restaurant some free coverage in a local paper is to offer up your services to them. Offer them a competition where two lucky readers get to dine with you for free. To go one step further, why not give away a cooking class? Some local papers have a recipe in each edition. Find out if you can supply the recipe if they'll name-check the restaurant on the page. There are plenty of ways to get free coverage but you have to make sure you're not a nuisance to the journalists you need to write about you. Here are some tips for getting the media on your side:

- Invite them round to the restaurant for dinner. If you've met and spoken to them face-to-face they're far more likely to give you the time of day later on.

- Don't contact them too often. If you become a nuisance they may just start avoiding you.
- Don't contact them with irrelevant stories. It's important you tailor any press releases, stories or promotions to fit in with their publications and what their readers want to see.
- Find out when deadline day is. If you contact a journalist when they're about to go to press they're unlikely to have time for you. Find out when their publication goes out and contact them straight afterwards as this will be the time they're most likely to listen you.
- Write a good press release. Journalists receive endless quantities of them so you'll need to make yours stand out if you want a chance of it being read, let alone covered. Have a look at the Marketing and PR channel of Startups.co.uk for more details on how to write a winning press release.

➡ LISTINGS AND GUIDES

Getting yourself listed in a local directory doesn't have to cost anything. Most directories such as *Thomson* or the *Yellow Pages* will allow you to have a basic entry with the name of the restaurant, the address and phone number for free. However, if you want a bigger advert with more prominence you will have to pay.

There are other smaller and more regularly updated local guides and directories which are often put through letterboxes or left in public buildings such as doctors' surgeries, information centres or local authority properties. These come in both printed and online formats. The printed guides or directories will have details on how to get your restaurant listed within them. Online versions will also have details of how to list for free or how to pay for greater prominence. Examples include, thebestof.co.uk, Welovelocal.com and Toplocallistings.co.uk.

However, a spot or thumbs up in a restaurant guide book is likely to generate a hell of a lot more custom. The difference is, you don't have as much choice in the matter when it comes to getting into *Harden's* or *The Good Food Guide*.

It won't do any harm, and it's free, to submit your restaurant details to these guides. Let them know who you are and where you can be found, and you may just find one of the guide writers pays you a visit. If they like what they see, and eat, you could land yourself in the guide, and bag a whole load of new customers to boot.

Here's a list of guides you may want to get in touch with to let them know you're open for business:

- *The Good Food Guide*
- *The Michelin Guide*
- *Time Out Eating and Drinking*
- *Harden's Restaurants Guide*
- *Zagat*
- *AA Restaurant Guide*

However, people are increasingly turning to the internet for inspiration on where to eat. Toptable.co.uk is the biggest of the restaurant review and special offer sites. Started by Karen Hanton in 2000, the site has over a million users per month, all looking for somewhere to eat. The site works by listing thousands of restaurants, and offers the restaurateur the opportunity to let customers book a table through the site. The incentive for customers to book is they build up reward points the more times they book via the site. You can also list any promotions or special offers against your restaurant profile. The service is free to sign up to and you'll pay a £2 fee for each diner that comes via a toptable booking.

To list your restaurant on toptable.co.uk call 020 7299 2945 or email lucy.taylor@toptable.co.uk.

Another site you may want to have your restaurant featured on is TrustedPlaces.com, a social networking site where members of the public put up personal reviews of restaurants, bars and pubs they visit. The eateries featured then build up a ranking as voted for by the public.

There are plenty of other online review and listings sites dedicated to the restaurant industry. It's a good idea to check out the ones specific to your area and make sure you're listed on all of those too.

➡ ONLINE MARKETING

You don't have to restrict yourself to being listed on other websites. If fact, you should make a point of creating your own, even if it's just one page with your restaurant name, address, opening hours and contact details. Nearly half of small businesses still have no online presence despite the fact that there's a whole generation of people out there who find almost all their information online. For a basic site, you don't even have to pay for it, and can have it up and running in a couple of hours. There are a number of free services out there such as Microsoft's Office Live, or BT's Tradespace, which give you free site you can create and update yourself as often as you want.

Visit www.smallbusiness.officelive.com or www.bttradespace.com and you get yourself an instant web presence without spending a single penny.

While these kind of services are great for giving you a basic web presence, if you want something a bit more flashy you'll probably need to get the professionals on board. It's not enough for your website to have a catchy domain name and some interesting content. People need to be instantly engaged when they land on a page, and much of that will stem from design, layout and how easy it is to navigate between, and find, different content. Depending on the size and scope of your restaurant you may find you don't need to hire expensive web designers when you first get started. Bear in mind that your domain name is just an address, and you can change the look and feel of your site as many times as you want. Basically you'll want to strike a balance between a site that looks good, gets users to return and doesn't cost the earth to build. Shop around for the best deal, perhaps even get companies to tender for the job based on a list of your requirements.

There are obvious details to put on the site such as contact details and where you're located but consider also putting a sample menu, as well as any current promotions up. Some photographs of the outside and inside of the restaurant can also be attractive to new customers who want to scope it out before they visit for the first time. To give the restaurant some background why not put a bit of a story online too. Tell your customers about yourself and your staff. Writing a regular blog can also do wonders to build a regular following and can also get your restaurant higher up in search engine rankings.

Another way of marketing your business online is to keep your customers informed with email or e-newsletter updates. If you leave a feedback card on tables you can ask customers for permission to email them with any news or offers. You can also have a sign-up form on your website where they can opt in to any updates. Use this marketing tool sparingly though. Customers don't want to be inundated with junk mail.

FROM THE EXPERTS:
Robin Rowland, Yo! Sushi

'We have about 250,000 people who opt into our database and whenever we do a special offer the uptake is quite extraordinary. But we don't do it very often. We're very selective with our discounting and this works incredibly well for us.'

Things to remember:

- Have a clear and defined marketing strategy before you start spending your budget.

- Think carefully about what kind of promotions you offer and apply them to your slower days or times.

- Use PR sparingly but effectively. Don't become a nuisance to journalists.

- Send your details off to guide books. They might pay you a visit.

- Get yourself some web presence. However basic it is, you must be online in some form.

Business development

Business development

Y ou may not be considering what's next for your restaurant at this stage. Perhaps the challenge of getting one site up and running is all you have the energy for at the moment. However, if you want to grow your business by a substantial amount, you're going to have to look at other options.

Expanding your business doesn't necessarily mean opening another restaurant; it could mean you start offering outside catering or home deliveries, or even open a shop within your restaurant selling branded products. If your plans include further expansion and you have confidence in your business model you could consider franchising or opening a second restaurant. You may want to reap the benefits of your hard work though by selling it on or even floating your business on the stock market.

In this chapter we'll cover:

- Catering
- Deliveries
- Cooking classes
- Retail ideas
- Franchising
- Opening a second restaurant
- Floating on the stock market
- Selling your business
- Passing your restaurant on

ALTERNATIVE IDEAS

Outside catering

The idea of catering for functions and private parties may seem impossible to you. If your kitchen is working at full capacity all day, every day, then there probably isn't the time or the space to entertain the option. However, if you experience dramatic fluctuations in seasonal trade, or have certain days or periods where trade is slow and your kitchen and staff have the capacity to take on some extra work, you may want to supplement your restaurant's revenue by doing outside catering.

The first thing you'll need to consider is whether you have the capacity, both in kitchen size and staff resources. If you don't, then that shouldn't stop you introducing a catering arm of the business altogether. You can always take on a separate kitchen and staff solely for the purpose of catering for events, and use your restaurant's name and customer base to promote it. Startups.co.uk has a full guide solely dedicated to setting up a catering business which you should read if you're considering this option.

Tips for setting up a catering arm to your restaurant

- Do plenty of analysis on both the customer demand for the service and existing competition.
- Don't take on the extra catering work at the expense of the restaurant running smoothly. You should only consider it if you can do both to an excellent standard.
- Make sure you set up secure payment terms and contracts with your customers. As a restaurateur you may be used to being paid promptly at the end of a meal. Payment for catering jobs is not always instant.
- Make sure any vehicle you use for transporting food abides by minimum legal requirements, which can be found in the Food Standards Agency booklet Safer Food, Better Business. You can download this at www.food.gov.uk.

If you do decide to branch out into catering, you will need to either add it to your existing one, or create a whole new business plan detailing who your customers will be, what your plans for promoting the service are, and what kind of pricing structure you'll follow. Essentially you'll be starting another business within your own, which will need careful consideration, and require a return to the drawing board in much the same way as when you wrote your restaurant's business plan.

Delivery service

Whether you decide to offer a delivery service will be dependent on the type of food you serve. Haute cuisine doesn't fare too well on the back of a moped and therefore won't be a suitable type of food to deliver to your customers. However, many types of food have a long history of being delivered. Many ethnic restaurants such as Chinese, Thai and Indian allow customers to enjoy the food without leaving their homes, and of course there's the staple pizza delivery guy. The last few years have seen a rise in the more traditional and authentic pizzerias offering a delivery option too, so the pizza box isn't just confined to the likes of Domino's and Pizza Hut.

Once you've established whether or not your food can survive travelling, you'll need to make a decision on how you'll absorb the extra costs involved in delivering. On the one hand you're selling items from your menu without the expense of waiting on customers. However, you now have to consider the cost of getting it to them, which involves packaging the food, the cost of a vehicle and its fuel as well as the extra staff resources.

Go back to your menu pricing formulas. Add in the extra costs associated with delivering and work out whether or not it's cost-effective to do so. If you decide it is, and this could involve a small delivery charge of a few pounds, you'll then need to establish some delivery procedures.

> ## ✦ TIP
> Determine your delivery radius by working out how long the food can stay hot and edible in the back of a car or bike. Be strict about it. There's no point telling your customers you can deliver five miles away if the food only maintains its quality for two.

Next you'll need to decide who's responsible for delivering the food. Are you prepared to hire a dedicated delivery person? This will only be cost-effective if you're getting a constant stream of orders throughout your opening times, otherwise you'll just be paying them to sit around. One way of testing the waters for a delivery service is to offer a takeaway service first. Inform your diners that they can also order food to go and see if there's much interest in the service. If people are calling up or coming in to order a takeaway and asking if you deliver, you'll be able to gauge whether or not it's worth taking on a delivery person.

Delicatessen/retail section

 FROM THE EXPERTS:
Simon Kossoff, Carluccio's

'Our shop section accounts for 20% of our turnover throughout the year but it climbs to about 50% at Christmas. Every Christmas I have this feeling that it's much easier to give someone a gift box and take £25 from them than it is to serve two people a three course meal. I get that sense every year. Unfortunately we can only do it at Christmas and a little at Easter. As an average it's 20% so it's not insignificant. In a restaurant you're faced with people walking in and saying "table for two please". In Carluccio's, they can wander in, have a look in the shop and browse around.'

The deli and retail section provided Carluccio's with its own unique selling proposition and contributed greatly to the overall turnover of the business. Space may not allow for a retail arm of your restaurant, but if it does it's an option to consider for increasing your revenue.

There are essentially two types of products you can sell in the retail arm of a restaurant: speciality products which relate to the type of food you serve, or products branded to your restaurant. Branded products could include cooking and table sauces, confectionary and condiments. You could also choose to have non-food items with your brand or logo on such as linens, aprons, crockery or glasses.

If you choose to sell speciality products, effectively turning part of your restaurant into a delicatessen, they'll need to be premium or luxury offerings. Customers aren't going to visit your restaurant and spend £12 on a bottle of balsamic vinegar they can buy in their local supermarket. However, if you can stock hard-to-find or rare delicacies you can attract customers who don't even dine in your restaurant.

Start small, stocking a few products for sale and decide whether or not there's a market for them. If you jump straight in and cordon off a whole section of the restaurant for retail then find your customers aren't willing to buy, you may end up losing revenue from a reduction in table space.

IN MY EXPERIENCE:
Lisa Tse, Sweet Mandarin

'Our next goal is to launch a range of branded sauces in the supermarkets. Since opening we've got a lot more savvy about costing, marketing and growing the business and we're determined to make Sweet Mandarin into a multi-platform brand.'

Cookery classes

Offering cookery classes is a great way to make the most of slow periods. If you simply don't do enough trade on a Monday evening, or lunchtimes just aren't pulling in the punters, why not open up your kitchen to a few willing students?

You'll need to think carefully about your pricing strategy for these classes. In the same way that you price up you menu, you should take into account the cost of any ingredients you use, energy you consume and staff costs associated with each lesson. You need to price the classes high enough to cover all this but also give you enough profit to make it worth your while. Anything less than £30 per person, per hour won't give you much of a return for the effort involved. In terms of a maximum cost, the sky's the limit depending on your restaurant's reputation, the type of area you're in and how much money your customer's are willing to pay for the experience.

If you don't plan to run the classes yourself, you'll need to talk it over with your chef to determine whether or not it's something they're willing or even capable of doing. Just because somebody is a genius in the kitchen, that doesn't automatically give them the skills to teach effectively. Your customers will attend to learn and pick up new skills, but the majority of people will attend because they'll expect a fun and entertaining experience.

TIP

Keep your classes small enough for each student to get personal attention. Aside from the obvious space restrictions you'll have in your kitchen, you don't want too many people there at once as it will be too difficult to manage. If your students don't feel like they're getting personal tuition, they might as well be watching a cookery programme at home. Try and keep numbers to a maximum of four people per teacher.

➡ ROLLING OUT THE CONCEPT

Opening your second restaurant

You may not be considering the prospect of a second restaurant at this stage. The effort involved in starting the first one may have left you exhausted. However, if you're looking to start again, or to add to the success of your first restaurant, you should think just as carefully, and be as thorough in your planning for a second site.

FROM THE EXPERTS:
Robin Rowland, Yo! Sushi

'The hardest growth point is taking a business from about four restaurants to more. When I took over the business we had eight restaurants that weren't contributing on top of four successful ones. My job was to unpick that, get rid of three bars and three restaurants and at the same time, add another two. I knew I could grow the business but it would have to go through a difficult time before it became profitable.'

Although difficult in many respects, such as splitting your time even further, managing more staff and having more to juggle, starting a second restaurant is a lot easier for a number of reasons. Firstly, you won't be making the same mistakes that you had to learn from with the first venture. All the issues that may have held up or hindered your first opening should be avoidable this time round.

You'll already have made contacts in terms of suppliers, who should be happy to negotiate deals if you up your orders with them to cater for both restaurants. Talk to them before you start your planning for the second restaurant, and ask what kind of deals they can offer you if you double your purchases. This kind of discounting may help you with your financial planning.

In terms of funding the second restaurant, you may have made enough profit from the first site to expand either with your own funds or a loan. If you go with investors they'll want to see evidence of success with the first venture, so your records should be in pristine order. See the section further on in the chapter on preparing your business for a sale to get a feel for the kind of record keeping investors will want to see.

IN MY EXPERIENCE:

Geetie Singh, The Duke of Cambridge

'People are always talking about growth and taking the business forward, but there comes a point when it's not about growth. It's about maintaining what you've got and retaining your position in the market. Moving the business forward for me is about looking at food fashion, making my supply chain more sustainable, and keeping the pub up-to-date.'

It's important to consider at this stage whether you really want the responsibility of a second restaurant too. Think long and hard about whether you're really up to it. Spreading yourself too thin can not only mean your second restaurant suffers, but it could have a knock-on effect on your original business if you take your eye off the ball. You'll need to make sure both restaurants have a solid team in place, with people you can trust to look after each site when you're not there. Only if you're confident either restaurant can survive without you there all the time to watch over things are you ready to branch out and open a second business.

FRANCHISING

What is it?

If you've created a successful new restaurant concept you may feel it has the potential to work really well as a chain. However, to do this you'll need heavy investment and a lot of hard work. One option for growing your business into a chain without running each site yourself is to turn the concept into a franchise.

A franchise is a successful business blueprint which you can then sell to other people. The franchisees will finance and manage the business, but use the brand, identity and concept you've created. The most famous example of any franchise is probably McDonald's. Other well-known examples in the UK include Domino's Pizza and Ed's Easy Diner.

How does it work?

If you want to franchise your restaurant you need to collate a complete business package or manual. Your franchisee buys this from you, but must agree to trade under your company name and abide by whatever trading methods you specify. You can stipulate that all stock or ingredients must be bought from you, or a particular supplier. You can also request additional items to be purchased from you including staff uniforms, furniture and menus etc. How much of this is included in your initial fee and package is down to you and the contract you draw up with your franchisees.

The contract between you and your franchisee is very important. It stipulates what ongoing financial obligations they owe to you, and specifies exactly how much influence or control you have over the way they run the restaurant. However, the franchisee will also require some assurances too. They'll want to know how much support they'll get from you in setting up the business and its ongoing management. They'll probably also expect a degree of marketing to be done by you on the overall brand.

You need to decide how much you want to charge for the initial licensing of the concept. Most franchise companies charge somewhere in the region of a couple of thousand pounds to buy the franchise so that franchisees can afford the start-up capital to get the restaurant up and running. You will then receive ongoing revenue from a share of the turnover of each business. You can also make money from a markup on anything you sell to your franchisees.

If you decide to franchise your business the first thing you need to do is go back to the drawing board in terms of research. You need to think long and hard about whether or not your concept is suited to franchising. If you're meticulous about quality control then a franchise may not be the best option for you. However, if you've created a concept that you feel can be successfully managed by others then it's definitely an option to consider.

The British Franchise Association (www.thebfa.org) can give you lots of help and advice in getting your concept off the ground. It's a good idea to contact the organisation early on in your planning stage. There's also a whole section dedicated to franchising information on Startups.co.uk. You can find useful information on franchising as well as list your own restaurant on the site so potential franchisees can contact you.

Useful franchise resources

The British Franchise Association
www.thebfa.org
01865 379892

FranchiseInfo
www.franinfo.co.uk

How2Franchise
www.how2franchise.co.uk

UK franchise directory
www.theukfranchisedirectory.net

FROM THE EXPERTS:
Robin Rowland, Yo! Sushi

'We chose a franchise route for taking Yo! Sushi to other countries. In my opinion you're off your rocker if you think you can make money overseas without help out there. I've seen so many companies arrogant enough to think they can do it with a great business model, but you can't do it without a reputation, an absolute knowledge of property and the right team out there.'

Attracting franchisees

To make a substantial amount from a franchise concept you need to have enough franchisees. Remember, it's only a share of the profits you'll be getting from each business. Your franchisees will need to be able to keep the majority of the revenue, otherwise what's in it for them? To gain enough franchisees you need to have an attractive package and market it well. Here are a few tips:

- Your initial fee and ongoing royalties need to be low enough to be affordable and attractive to potential franchisees. However, you need to strike a balance between affordable for them, and profitable for you.
- Your business should also be well established, secure and have an excellent reputation before you even think about franchising. You need to be able to prove to your potential franchisees that it's a business concept worth investing in. The only way to do that is to hone your own operation into a finely tuned concept.
- You need to offer enough management support. It's no good just throwing in the rights to the restaurant name and a few uniforms. You need a thorough business manual with instructions on everything from recipes and customer service to table layouts and prices.
- You need to show a willingness to market and develop the business from central office. Franchisees are buying into a brand name, with all the security and customer recognition that offers.
- You need to prove you're willing to protect the brand which means choosing your franchisees carefully. You can't just hand out the licence to anyone willing to stump up the cash. One bad franchise brings down the reputation of all of them, and your hard-working franchisees will want reassurance that their business isn't being undermined by unsuccessful branches.

➡ FLOATING

Why float?

Floating on the stock market is only really an option if your restaurant has become a large chain. It takes a lot of work to prepare a company for any of the UK's stock markets, of which there are three – the Stock Exchange's Main Market, the Alternative Investment Market (AIM) and Plus. Carluccio's didn't float on AIM until it had 25 restaurants, and had already been trading for half a decade. This should give you an idea of the kind of level you need to reach with your restaurant business before you can even consider a flotation.

When a company floats a percentage of the business is sold off in shares which investors can then buy. Most businesses deicide to float so they can release a substantial amount of capital, perhaps for expansion of the business, without selling it on to another company or individual. However, floating a business is an expensive and extremely time-consuming process, and not a decision any business owner enters into lightly.

The first thing you need to consider is whether your business has enough growth potential for investors to be interested in buying shares. You also need to consider whether your management team is capable of taking on such a mammoth task.

Pros and cons of floating

Pros

- You can raise a substantial amount of capital in one go.
- You can release money that you and your investors have invested.
- You gain more recognition for your company.
- You can offer shares to employees as an incentive.

Cons

- There are substantial fees and ongoing costs associated with floating.
- There is a heavy administrative burden which you'll need to bring in outside help for.
- Your business will be at the mercy of market fluctuations.
- Your shareholders will expect decisions to be made in the best interests of their investments rather than you as the founder. You also risk being removed from the board if they're unhappy with your management.
- There is increased regulatory control once you've floated.

Main market

The main market is for really big companies and probably wouldn't be an option for your business unless you struck gold with your restaurant concept. You also need to have been trading for at least three years. The fees are highest for the Main Market out of all three options for floating, and you are also required to float at least a quarter of your company's equity. However, the Main Market is the best known and the most publicised and therefore reaches the widest possible range of potential investors.

AIM

Unlike the Main Market, you don't need prior trading history to float on the AIM. There's also less of a regulatory burden, lower fees and no minimum percentage for the amount of shares you have to sell off. AIM is the option Simon Kossoff chose for Carluccio's when he wanted to secure an exit for his early investors without selling the company via a trade sale.

PLUS

The PLUS market is aimed at even smaller companies – those that are looking to release up to £10m of capital. Although the market is still regulated, it's not as stringent as the Main Market or AIM. The costs associated with PLUS are also much lower. However, on the down side, it does not have as wide an audience and therefore not such a big pool of potential investors.

FROM THE EXPERTS:
Simon Kossoff, Carluccio's

'In December 2005 we floated on AIM. Part of our agreement with our original investors was that we'd find them an exit in five years time. They'd been very supportive and loved business but when we got past six years there was a sense that we had to live up to our promise. We could have sold Carluccio's to another restaurateur or a private equity company but I felt the management team still had more to do. I felt at least with the flotation we were in still control of our own destiny and not at the hands of a single owner.'

➡ SELLING OR EXITING THE BUSINESS

Should you sell?

There are many reasons why you may feel like selling your restaurant. You may want to cash in on the financial success of what you've built by accepting an offer from another restaurateur. Or perhaps you want to move on, either to a different location or because of family or personal commitments. Or maybe you just want to retire. Building up a successful business that can be sold on may have been your intention from the very beginning. Whatever your reasons for wanting to sell, there are plenty of things to consider before you do so.

Another reason you may consider selling your business is if it's not performing as well as expected. If your restaurant is in financial difficulty a sale could prove tricky. However, it may be a way of recouping some of your investment without closing it down altogether. If this is the case, you should prepare yourself for price offers that don't reflect the amount of time, effort and money you've put into the business.

IN MY EXPERIENCE:

Shevonne Bennett, Brown Sugar

'I sold the original business so that I could look for a better venue and give the place a complete rebrand, making it more mainstream. Where we were, the rent was just too high and despite having really good sales, our outgoings were too expensive and the landlord wouldn't negotiate.'

The most likely route for selling a single restaurant is in a trade sale to another restaurateur or business owner. However, if the restaurant you've built up is big and profitable enough, you may find that a private equity buyer or venture capital firm is interested.

Selling your business takes a lot of planning. It's not as simple as handing over the keys in exchange for a cheque. It needs to be in a sale-ready state which means making sure all your finances are in immaculate order. The same goes for the whole business operation. The books need to have been gone through with a fine toothcomb. Needless to say, all tax and official records must be completely up-to-date. You'll also need to be able to produce evidence of cashflow, turnover and profits. This will apply to the financial history of the business as well as how it's currently performing and what your projections for the future are.

Before you even think about selling your business it's a good idea to take on some help with the sale in the form of an accountant and a solicitor. Your accountant should be able to prepare the business accountants for a sale. You may already have an accountant, but if they are not experienced when it comes to business sales it's advisable to bring somebody on board who is. Your solicitor will be the one responsible for drafting sale agreements and will negotiate with your buyer and their legal advisors if necessary.

Valuing your business

There are so many different factors that affect the value of your business and your current turnover and profit is just one part of that. Essentially your business is only worth what buyers are willing to pay. This can be affected by things that are beyond your control such as the current state of the economy, the value of property in the area and what similar businesses are going on the market for.

However, there are plenty more elements of your business that will have been shaped and controlled by you. These include:

- Financial history
- Current financial health
- The restaurant's reputation
- The restaurant's position within the community
- The business' potential for growth
- The quality of your team
- The contents and physical appearance of your restaurant

Part of presenting a valuation of your restaurant to potential buyers will involve preparing a sales memorandum. This will generally be produced in conjunction with your sales advisors – so your accountant and solicitor. The sales memorandum is a kind of marketing pitch which includes information on your company, and presents it in a favourable light in order to attract buyers. Information on the memorandum includes trading history, key financial figures and how these have fared during previous years. The memorandum will also have details on your premises and your employees.

Finding buyers

Potential buyers are everywhere. You may be able to target a competitor in your area who is keen to take over your business and expand their own. Or maybe you know someone who runs a similar business in another location who's keen to take on an extra business. If you're considering selling your restaurant you may want to return to good old-fashioned networking to find potential buyers. You can even look within your own team for a buyer. Perhaps one of your staff members is in a position to stump up the cash to take over your restaurant.

However, if you don't know someone personally who's in a position to buy your business you'll have to advertise that it's for sale. There are several trade magazines and business directories you can use to list your restaurant in. These include: *Daltons Business* (www.daltonsbusiness.com) and *Businesses For Sale* (www.businessesforsale.com).

Once you have some interested buyers that you feel are realistically in a position to take your restaurant over, you can have your advisors send them your sales memorandum. You don't have to meet all of your potential buyers at this stage, but obviously with a business such as a restaurant, it's likely they'll want to view it before making any kind of initial offer. If you

> ### ✦ TIP
> It's a good idea to draw up a non-disclosure agreement for all prospective buyers to sign. This way, even if you have to reveal confidential company information to them, you can be confident they won't reveal it to anyone else.

have several interested buyers, the next stage will be to start holding meetings with them.

Choosing a buyer should never just be a question of accepting the highest bid. You should also consider how your buyer is willing to structure the sale, to what extent they are planning to change or build on what you've already developed and what you both agree is an acceptable timetable for finalising the sale.

Once you've agreed a sale with your buyer it will then be subject to the process of due diligence. This is where the buyer engages in a thorough inspection of the business, covering things such as financial records, staff agreements, customer and supplier relationships, premises, legal and tax obligations and intellectual property.

Your responsibility

If you're selling your restaurant you need to be aware of Transfer of Undertakings (Protection of Employment) Regulations 2006, also known as TUPE. You'll be familiar with these regulations if you bought your business from someone else. The basis of these regulations is that when a business changes hands, the new employer is not allowed to change the terms of employment the existing members of staff currently have. All your employees, or at least a representative of them, should also be consulted and informed regarding the sale of your business.

When you sell a business you also have a responsibility to the taxman to consider. Entrepreneurs are subject to Capital Gains Tax (CGT) when they sell off business assets. In 2008 changes to CGT came into force which included the abolition of Taper Relief which allowed assets held for more than two years to enjoy a reduced rate of 10%. Gains made on the disposal of business assets are now charged at a flat rate of 18%. There are a few exceptions however. If your gains are equal to, or less than, the annual exempt amount, you may not have to pay CGT. The annual exempt amount for 2008/09 is £9,600. Another exemption applies where your lifetime gains do not exceed £1m. This is called entrepreneurs' relief, and it charges gains at a reduced rate of 10%. Any gains after your first £1m are charged at 18%.

There are other allowances and exemptions to CGT which is why it is advisable to seek professional advice from a specialised accountant or solicitor before you sell your business.

Passing the business on

If you decide you want to sell the business to a friend or relative, the process above will still apply. However, you may want to pass the business on, perhaps to a son or daughter, without receiving payment for it. The first thing you need to consider is whether the person you've earmarked for taking over the restaurant is really suited to doing so. If they've worked with you in the restaurant, it should be pretty apparent whether or not they're capable of taking over all your responsibilities. However, if they don't have the right level of experience, and we've established by now that running a restaurant is definitely not a business anyone can come along and make a success of, you could find all your hard work goes out the door as soon as you hand over the keys.

As well as assessing whether or not your successor is capable of taking over the business, you also need to establish if they even want to. Running a restaurant takes passion and dedication and if you pass the business on to someone who's taken it over out of a sense of obligation, your restaurant could soon suffer the consequences. Another possible problem, particularly when passing a business on to offspring is making a decision about who has overall control and responsibility. If you have more than one child, you may want them both to share in the financial success of the business, but conflict could arise if you haven't established from the outset who has overall control when it comes to management decisions.

The same goes for your own involvement. How much day-to-day involvement do you still want, and will whoever you've passed the business on to be comfortable with that? It's no good handing over the responsibility and hard work of the restaurant management to somebody, only to enforce your own decisions on the business. If you really want to pass the business on to somebody else, you need to be willing to let go of the reins.

Things to remember:

- Business development isn't just about increasing your profits. It's also about maintaining quality and improving what you've already built.

- Don't take on extra responsibility, such as catering or retail commitments, if it puts the health of the restaurant at risk.

- Don't consider a second restaurant until you feel you can be away from your first one without it collapsing.

- Franchising demands a flawless original business model. Don't consider this route until you've achieve one.

- Make sure you take professional advice before beginning a transfer or sale of the restaurant.

Appendices

SWOT analysis table

Strengths		Weaknesses
• Why should you succeed? • What do you do well? • Why do customers say they enjoy doing bwness with you? • What distinct advantages does your company offer? • What are your USPs?		• What could be improved about the business? • Is the market strong enough? • Do you have enough/good enough staff on board? • Are your management skills up to scratch? • Do you have enough finance to make it work? • What stumbling blocks do you continue to encounter? • What does your company do that can be improved? • What should be avoided? • What do your competitors do better than you?
	S	**W**
Opportunities	**O**	**T** **Threats**
• Where are the openings for your business? • Has the market significantly changed recently? • What customer needs are not being met by your competitors?		• What is your competition doing that could take business away from you or stunt your company's growth? • How might your competitors react to any moves you make? • What trends in the market do you see that could wipe you out or make your business obsolete? • Might technology changes threaten your products or services? Or your job? • Do you have a stable relationship with suppliers and partners?

Example market analysis table for a new Italian restaurant on a busy town high street

Competitors	Number of years established	Price bracket (eg cost of main meal)	Their strengths	Their weaknesses	Your USPs/what you offer the market
Small family run restaurant	5	£10	Good homemade food	Décor is tired and restaurant does not look inviting	Fresh, inviting décor, with fresh, delicious food
Pizza chain restaurant	8	£13	Well established and good reputation for standard Italian food	Lacking in character? Impersonal service	Well-trained, attentive waiting staff. Discount on second visit
High-end, posh eatery	3	£20	The high-end choice, good romantic atmosphere, nice décor. Intricate, well presented food	Only busy at weekends, appeals to a very niche market	Aim to create the same friendly atmosphere, but at a lower cost and less fussy food to appeal to more people.

Financial budget plan

Startup costs	Estimated cost
Business registration fees	
Initial stock	
Rent deposits	
Down payments on property	
Down payments on equipment	
Restaurant-fitting costs	
Utility set up fees	
Operating costs	
Your salary	
Staff salaries	
Rent or mortgage payments	
Telecommunications	
Utlities	
Stock	
Storage	
Distribution	
Promotion	
Loan payments	
Office supplies	
Maintenance	
Professional services (ie accountancy fees)	

Cash Flow Forecast

	Month 1	Month 2	Month 3	Month 4	Month 5	Month 6	Month 7	Month 8	Month 9	Month 10	Month 11	Month 12	YTD
Receipts													
Debtors	8,297	8,572	6,798	7,569	7,719	8,071	7,765	7,175	6,179	7,637	5,978	7,173	88,933
Cash	276	421	1,403	1,386	874	835	1,142	1,607	1,946	818	2,036	918	13,662
TOTAL RECEIPTS	8,573	8,993	8,201	8,955	8,593	8,906	8,907	8,782	8,125	8,455	8,014	8,091	102,595
Payments													
Purchases	1,687	1,967	2,173	2,469	2,284	2,982	2,642	2,381	2,974	3,129	2,367	2,894	29,949
Rent	2,160	-	-	2,160	-	-	2,160	-	-	2,160	-	-	8,640
Rates & utilities	528	528	528	528	528	528	528	528	528	528	528	528	6,336
Telephone	-	-	509	-	-	521	-	-	539	-	-	517	2,086
Wages & Salaries	2,750	2,750	2,750	2,750	2,750	2,750	2,750	2,750	2,750	2,750	2,750	2,750	33,000
PAYE	1,018	1,018	1,018	1,018	1,018	1,018	1,018	1,018	1,018	1,018	1,018	1,018	12,216
VAT	102	-	-	47	-	-	156	-	-	174	-	-	479
TOTAL Payments	8,245	6,263	6,978	8,972	6,580	7,799	9,254	6,677	7,809	9,759	6,663	7,707	92,706
NET OPERATING CASH FLOW	328	2,730	1,223	(17)	2,013	1,107	(347)	2,105	316	(1,304)	1,351	384	9,889
Fixed Asset purchases	539				1,299				3,675				5,513
Loan repayments	-												-
Net cash inflow/(outflow)	(211)	2,730	1,223	(17)	714	1,107	(347)	2,105	(3,359)	(1,304)	1,351	384	4,376
OPENING BANK BALANCE	1,628	1,417	4,147	5,370	5,353	6,067	7,174	6,827	8,932	5,573	4,269	5,620	1,628
CLOSING BANK BALANCE	1,417	4,147	5,370	5,353	6,067	7,174	6,827	8,932	5,573	4,269	5,620	6,004	6,004

Profit & loss example

For month ended 30/06/2008

	£	£
Sales/turnover		**60,894**
Opening stock (1st of Month)	3,000	
Add purchases made	24,253	
	27,253	
Less closing stock (30/31st of month)	4,278	
Cost of goods sold	31,531	
Direct labour costs	7,364	
		38,895
Gross Profit		**29,363**
Overheads		
Rent and rates	3,294	
Heat, light and power	783	
Insurance	106	
Indirect wages and salaries	7,296	
Marketing costs	571	
Printing, stationery and consumables	1,951	
Computer costs	758	
Telephone	939	
Depreciation of assets	3,697	
Legal and professional fees	750	
Bank and finance charges	264	
		20,409
Net Profit Before Tax		**8,954**

Example shift schedule

Shift schedule week ending: 27/07/2008

Employee	MON	TUES	WED	THURS	FRI	SAT	SUN	TOTAL HOURS
FLOOR SUPERVISOR 1	CLOSED	17.00 – 2300	17.00 – 2300	17.00 – 2300		20.00–12.30	20.00–11.30	
FLOOR SUPERVISOR 2	CLOSED				18.00 –12.30	13.00 – 18.00	13.00 – 18.00	
Waiting Staff 1	CLOSED		17.00 – 2300		17.00–12.30	18.00 –12.30	20.00–11.30	
Waiting Staff 2	CLOSED	17.00 – 2300		17.00 – 2300	17.00–12.30	18.00 –12.30		
Waiting Staff 3	CLOSED				19.00–12.30	13.00 – 18.00	13.00 – 18.00	
Head Chef 1	CLOSED	17.00 – 2300		17.00 – 2300		12.00–18.00	18.00 –12.00	
Head Chef 2	CLOSED		17.00 – 2300		18.00 –12.00	18.00 –12.00	12.00–18.00	
Commis Chef 1	CLOSED	12.00–14.00	12.00–14.00	12.00–14.00	18.00 –12.00	18.00 –12.00	12.00–18.00	
Commis Chef 2	CLOSED	17.00 – 2300	17.00 – 2300	17.00 – 2300	12.00–14.00	12.00–14.00	12.00–14.00	
Kitchen Porter/Cleaner	CLOSED	18.00–23.00	18.00–23.00	18.00–23.00	18.00 –12.00	14.00–23.00	14.00–10.00	
GENERAL MANANGER	12.00–19.00	12.00–19.00	12.00–19.00	12.00–19.00	12.00–19.00			

Shift schedule is subject to change for group bookings so please check shift schedule each shift

Thank you

Index